D0289208

CHILDREN'S GUIDE TO LONDON

CHILDREN'S GUIDE TO LONDON

By Christopher Pick

Illustrated by Ian Ribbons

CADOGAN BOOKS
LONDON

For Alison, with love

First published 1985
© Christopher Pick 1985
Illustrations © Ian Ribbons 1985

ISBN 0 946313 31 8

No part of this book may be reproduced in
any form without permission of the publisher

Published by Cadogan Books Ltd.
16 Lower Marsh, London SE1
(Holding Company – Metal Bulletin PLC)

Phototypeset on Linotron 101 in 10 on 11pt Ehrhardt
by Photocomp Ltd, Birmingham

Printed and bound in Great Britain by
Richard Clay PLC, Bungay, Suffolk

INTRODUCTION

I sometimes think that two quite distinct Londons co-exist. There is tourist London – a London that all too often seems to consist of not much more than the crush in front of Buckingham Palace when the Guard is being changed, the long, slow queue round the Tower of London, and the obligatory visit to Carnaby Street. And then – not miles away in a separate part of town but literally side by side – there is what I think of as *real* London: a living capital city of almost inexhaustible variety and excitement, with a vivid history that speaks out of the buildings and streets, and with an equally vibrant, cosmopolitan life that continues day by day.

I have loved London for as long as I can remember – and I have always especially loved walking around, exploring byways and back streets as well as highways, and enjoying the constant surprises and changes of scene that the city offers. This book is a product of that love, and in particular of my attempts in recent years to explain and justify my enthusiasms to my daughter as we have explored London together.

Thirteen walks are described in this book – or rather, to be absolutely accurate, twelve walks proper and one boat trip down the Thames to Greenwich. The majority are in central London (by which I mean the area bounded roughly by Camden Town, Tower Bridge, the south bank of the Thames in Southwark and Notting Hill Gate), although there are two excursions further afield: to Greenwich, and to Hampstead and Highgate.

I have deliberately centred each route on a reasonably well-known area that visitors to London, and native Londoners themselves as well, would want to visit. But then I have tried to get off the beaten track and behind the well-worn tourist trails in order to point out the details and quirks that add fun and life to the city, and the buildings and monuments and squares that give it its special character. I have also incorporated in each route, and described, as many museums and other 'attractions' of especial interest to children (whether they are 6 or 14) as possible.

The majority of walks are quite short, and can be completed in no more than a couple of hours, although additional time must be allowed for museum visits. Even so, there is no reason why, if you have a slow-moving toddler in tow, you should not tackle as little as a ½ mile. The maps show all the Underground stations passed *en route*, so that joining or leaving a walk part-way through is quite simple. Since I know from experience how important these are, I have listed at the start of each walk the public lavatories passed, and have suggested a few reasonably priced cafés plus some pleasant spots to sit down for a few minutes, or longer if you have your own picnic with you. The bus routes and underground stations that serve the starting- and finishing-points of each walk are also given. Opening hours for museums along each route are also provided (assume that such organizations are closed on Christmas Day and Boxing Day).

The section on restaurants in London describes some of the capital's restaurants that make a positive attempt to welcome children and make them feel at home.

London, of course, has an unrivalled range of sporting, cultural and entertainment facilities of every kind. The reference section at the back of the book lists a selection that offer activities aimed at children and young people. Among the topics included are arts and drama workshops, children's theatres and cinemas, museums of all kinds, zoos and nature centres, sports centres and ice rinks. The scope of these listings has been widened to include the entire GLC area. This part of the book has been compiled from information supplied by each organization listed and by the individual London boroughs.

A book such as this is not written without incurring many debts. First of all I would like to thank the 'eaters-out' who compiled the data on which the restaurant section is based; the many museum curators, theatre administrators and others who readily responded to my questionnaire and in so doing provided the raw material for the reference section; and Cadogan Books, who took some of the administrative work off my hands. Thanks are also due to countless individuals and organizations all over the capital, too numerous to list here, who answered my queries and requests for information by letter and phone, and in person when I was working out the routes on the ground. I am especially grateful to the London Visitor & Convention Bureau for help in this respect. Mrs Pat Scott and the staff of Upper Norwood Public Library obtained books for me very promptly, which was a great help; and the fantastic view from behind the library, where the whole of central London lies spread out before you, never failed to provide inspiration every time I went to collect the books. Of the many books consulted, two must be singled out by name: *The Companion Guide to London* by David Piper (Collins 1964, sixth edition 1977) and *The London Encyclopaedia*, edited by Ben Weinreb and Christopher Hibbert (Macmillan 1983). Piper's beautifully written book is an inspiring guide that has opened my eyes to many things I might otherwise have missed, while the *Encyclopaedia* is a fascinating source of information on every aspect of the capital's life and history. I have left my biggest debt to last: to my wife Jenny and my daughter Alison, who both provided moral support at all times, and especially to Alison, who came with me on many explorations and set me right when my enthusiasms carried me too far.

Christopher Pick
West Norwood, London SE27
4 October 1985

PUBLISHER'S NOTE

While every attempt had been made to check the accuracy of the information contained in this book, no responsibility can be taken for any errors. When planning a visit, it is advisable to telephone an attraction in advance to check opening times etc.

CONTENTS

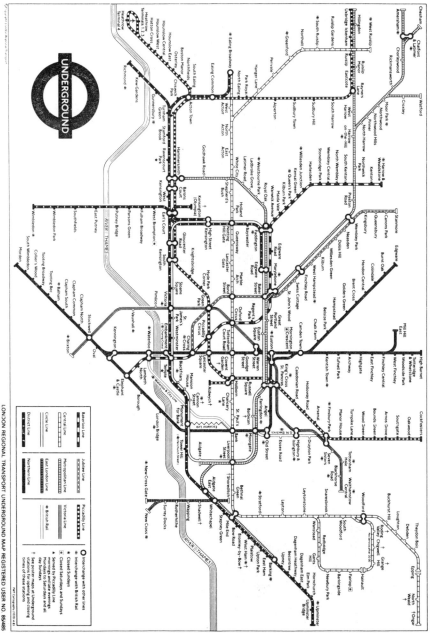

LONDON REGIONAL TRANSPORT UNDERGROUND MAP REGISTERED USER NO. 85/485

UNDERGROUND

2A

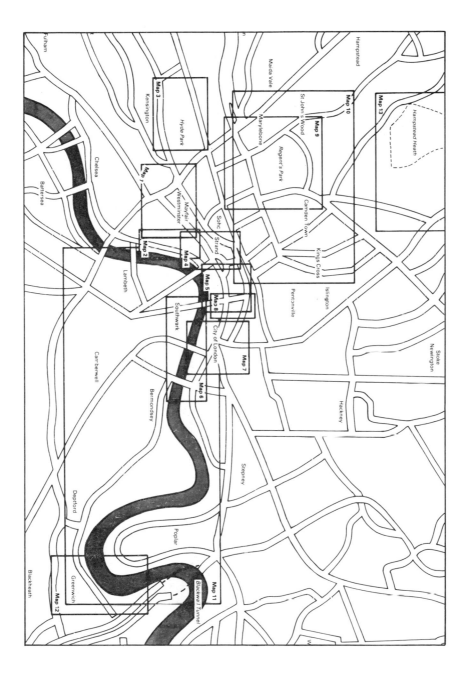

1   ROYAL LONDON

Start: Admiralty Arch, Trafalgar Square
Underground: Charing Cross
Buses: 1, 1A, 3, 6, 9, 11, 12, 13, 15, 23, 24, 29, 53,
     77, 77A, 88, 159, 170, 173

Finish: Wellington Museum, Hyde Park Corner
Underground: Hyde Park Corner
Buses: 2, 2B, 9, 14, 16, 19, 22, 25, 30, 36, 36B, 38,
     52, 52A, 55, 73, 74, 137, 500

Distance: 3·75 kilometres (2⅓ miles)

Places to sit down: St James's Park and Green Park

Lavatories: In parks, as shown on display maps

This walk could conveniently be combined with seeing the
Guard being changed (for times and places see end of
walk). But it is also very pleasant to do on its own at any
time of the day or early evening. At lunchtime you could

1

join London's office-workers enjoying their sandwiches in St James's Park, one of the loveliest of central London's parks, and maybe listen to a band playing in the bandstand.

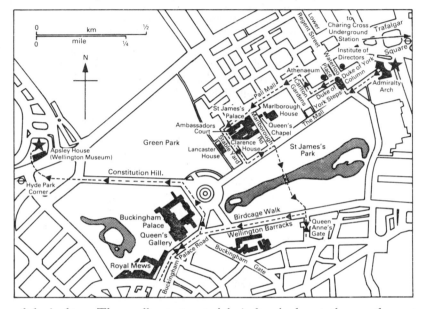

Admiralty Arch   The walk starts at Admiralty Arch, at the south-west corner of Trafalgar Square. It is not a place to linger, as all the traffic is channelled through the two side arches. (The central gates are only opened on ceremonial occasions.) The Arch – one of London's least inspiring or attractive monuments – forms part of the national memorial to Queen Victoria created a few years after her death in 1901. It takes its name from the Admiralty Building, a short way down Whitehall.

The Mall   Beyond the Arch, The Mall is also part of the memorial to Queen Victoria. The Mall and Pall Mall, part of which we will walk along presently, are easily confused. The original route named Pall Mall ran from Buckingham Palace to the village of Charing, where Trafalgar Square is now, and was a popular place for playing a croquet-like game called *paille-maille* (pronounced 'pell mell'). Players and coaches and horses tended to get in each others' way – the sportsmen could not see the ball for the clouds of dust the coaches threw up – and so in the early 1660s the present Pall Mall was built as a through route for travellers. The Mall then became one of the places where people of fashion promenaded. Finally, at the beginning of this century, the road now called The Mall was constructed a few yards to the left of the original Mall as part of the memorial to Queen Victoria. The original route remains as the gravel ride that runs from Duke of York Steps to Buckingham Palace.

Nowadays, The Mall is spoilt by heavy traffic moving too fast, and it only comes alive on ceremonial occasions when soldiers march and flags flutter in the breeze. Our route takes us along the right-hand side, in front of the façade of Carlton House Terrace and opposite The Citadel, a still top-secret building erected in the Second World War to provide bombproof accommodation for the Admiralty.

Duke of York Steps Turn right up Duke of York Steps. Frederick, Duke of York, the second son of George III, was the famous duke who marched his 10,000 men up to the top of the hill and then marched them down again. Our route goes up only, past the Duke of York Column. The duke stands 38 metres (124 feet) above ground level – high enough, it was said at the time, to keep him out of the way of his creditors (he died in 1827 owing no less than £2 million). The memorial was paid for by deducting a day's pay from every soldier: not a popular move.

You are now standing on what was once London's most sumptuous royal residence: Carlton House, built in the early 18th century and extended and improved at enormous expense about a century later by the Prince of Wales, who later became the Prince Regent and then George IV. Lower Regent Street, the road in front of you running gently uphill to Piccadilly Circus, was the final part of the grand processional route which the Prince, with his architect friend John Nash, planned to run from his park – Regent's Park (see walk 9) – down Regent Street to his palace.

A grand ball was held here in 1811 to mark the start of the Prince's Regency. But nine years later, when he succeeded to the throne, the new king decided that

Carlton House was not grand enough, and he embarked on the improvement of Buckingham Palace. His old home was pulled down, and Nash built Carlton House Terrace on the site.

London's Clubs

The streets round here are London's clubland. On the left-hand corner of Waterloo Place in front of you is the Athenaeum and on the right the Institute of Directors, which now occupies the building that used to belong to the United Services Club. Gentlemen's clubs are a unique British institution, at least on the scale at which they still function in London. The subscription is high (usually several hundred pounds a year); you must know several members to be elected; and women are not normally permitted to become members and in some clubs are still only allowed in certain parts of the building. Each club appeals to people with particular interests and occupations: the Athenaeum is mostly for bishops and professors, the Carlton for Conservative politicians, the Garrick for lawyers and media people.

Carlton House Terrace

From the top of the steps, we turn left along Carlton House Terrace, past the headquarters of the Royal Society – the country's, and one of the world's, most important scientific institutions – and into Carlton Gardens. At number 4 General de Gaulle set up the headquarters of the Free French forces in 1940 – the small band of French men and women who escaped from occupied France to continue the fight against Nazi Germany from England.

Just before number 4 turn right and walk past Wool House, where the International Wool Secretariat is, and then turn left into Pall Mall. Clubs along here are the Travellers, the Reform, the Army and Navy, the Royal Automobile and the United Oxford and Cambridge University.

Crown Passage on the right is a curiously ordinary alleyway amid all this Establishment grandeur, and has a couple of pleasant sandwich bars.

Marlborough House

The road widens at the entrance to Marlborough House, built between 1709 and 1711 for Sarah, Duchess of Marlborough, widow of the victor of the Battle of

Blenheim. Edward VII lived here while he was Prince of Wales. His son, who became George V, was born here, and George's consort Mary lived here after his death. The house has been used as the headquarters of the Commonwealth Secretariat, but will close at the end of 1985 for at least three years while major restoration work is carried out.

Queen's Chapel

The Queen's Chapel, on the left down Marlborough Road, can be visited if you attend morning service on Sundays between Easter and the end of July. Work on the chapel started in 1623 when it seemed that Charles I was going to marry the Infanta of Spain. When the marriage negotiations collapsed, work on the chapel ceased, and only resumed a few years later when Charles married Henrietta Maria. There arc royal pews and a splendid ceiling.

St James's Palace

On the other side of Marlborough Road stands St James's Palace. This has been a royal residence since Henry VIII's reign four and a half centuries ago, and from the end of the 17th century until 1837 was the principal official residence of the monarch. Foreign diplomats in London are still accredited to the Court of St James's, even though they are received in Buckingham Palace when they take up their appointment.

St James's is a complex building, and only a few parts are open to the public. Opposite the Queen's Chapel is Friary Court, where the accession of a new sovereign is proclaimed from the balcony. Behind Friary Court are the State Apartments, which are opened on special occasions such as royal weddings when gifts are displayed.

Lancaster House

Return to the corner of Pall Mall and Marlborough Road, walk along Cleveland Row, past the original Tudor gatehouse of the Palace and turn left into Stable Yard. The main building on the right is Lancaster House, nowadays used for government banquets, receptions and meetings. There are some sumptuous state rooms on the first floor. Lancaster House has not always been called Lancaster; previous names have included York (the building was commissioned by the Duke of York whose steps we climbed earlier) and Stafford, after the Marquess of Stafford who once owned it.

Chapel Royal
To the left of Stable Yard is Ambassadors Court, through which you pass on your way to the Chapel Royal. The public may attend Sunday morning services here between October and Good Friday. Charles I came to worship here on the morning of his execution, and then walked across St James's Park to Banqueting House (see walk 2), his dog running after him. Queen Victoria and Prince Albert were married in the Chapel in 1840.

Clarence House
Behind the high wall on the left side of Stable Yard Road is Clarence House, built in 1828 for the Duke of Clarence and now the home of the Queen Mother. The present Queen lived here for three years after her marriage in 1947, and Princess Anne was born here.

At the end of Stable Yard Road turn left into The Mall and walk alongside St James's Palace. The route of the original Mall is clearly visible (see above). The palace also contains the private apartments of the Duke and Duchess of Kent, and the offices of the Lord Chamberlain.

St James's Park
Now from pavements to the park. Our route crosses St James's Park by the main north-south path that starts opposite the junction of Marlborough Road and The Mall. The park is well worth exploiting, and there is a pleasant if rather pricey little refreshment pavilion called The Cake House near the north side of the lake at the Horse Guards end.

St James's Park has been a royal park since Henry VIII came to live in Whitehall (see walk 2), and that is still its official status, although it is administered by the Department of the Environment. Charles II extended the park and had it remodelled by Le Nôtre, the French landscape designer. George IV chose his friend John Nash to undertake yet another landscaping project, and he produced the park we enjoy today. Among the 45 species of birds found in the park – either resident all year round, or summer, winter or casual visitors – are pelicans, descendants of a pair donated by a Russian ambassador in the 17th century. At the east end of the lake is Duck Island (not open to the public) on which William III built himself a cabin for birdwatching.

Queen Anne's Gate On the far side of the park, cross Birdcage Walk and walk the few yards uphill into Queen Anne's Gate, where there is an almost perfect row of 18th-century houses. You can get a real sense here of how much of London used to look, if one can ignore the massive modern fortress of the Home Office behind.

Returning to Birdcage Walk, so called because James I had an aviary here, turn left and walk past the Guards' Chapel, totally rebuilt after it received a direct hit in the Second World War. The Wellington Barracks beyond (if you look carefully you can see signs to the NAAFI) are the headquarters of five regiments of Foot Guards. A Guards Museum is planned to open in about 1987. The Guards Shop sells books and other souvenirs.

Queen's Gallery Continue straight on at the end of Birdcage Walk along Buckingham Gate and then Buckingham Palace Road if you want to visit the Queen's Gallery or the Royal Mews. These are the only parts of Buckingham Palace to which the public is admitted. The Gallery stages major exhibitions of paintings, jewellery, etc. and was constructed on the site of the private chapel in the palace, which was bombed in 1940.

Royal Mews Some way on the right beyond the entrance to the Queen's Gallery is the entrance to the Royal Mews. The Royal Mews offer a fascinating glimpse of the day-to-day workings of one part of royal life. The Gold State Coach, which was built for George III's coronation and has been used at every succeeding coronation, is on view, along with other royal carriages and cars. About 20 of the Queen's carriage horses are stabled here. The visit is well worth while. After all, it's not every day that you get the chance to see some royal horse manure!

Almost opposite the entrance to the Royal Mews is the headquarters of the Girl Guides Association, where there is a well-stocked shop.

Buckingham Palace Return to the front of Buckingham Palace, where there are always crowds of people. Inside the palace there are about 600 rooms. A few of these are the private apartments of the Queen and the Duke of Edinburgh, Prince Andrew and Prince Edward. (Princess Anne also lives in the Palace when she is in London.) Most of the other rooms are the offices of the Royal Household, that is, the men and women who organize the Queen's affairs. The Royal Standard flies from the flagpole when the Queen is in residence, normally during most working weeks except in January, August and September, although she is away quite often on short trips around the UK and on state visits abroad.

Buckingham Palace is the most recent of London's royal residences. Buckingham House, the original mansion on this site, was completly redesigned in a grandiose and extremely costly plan devised by John Nash and the Prince Regent when he succeeded to the throne as George IV. In fact, both George and his brother William IV died before work was completed, and Queen Victoria had to endure ten years of improvements before the palace was comfortably habitable. The east front, which faces you as you stand by the railings, was added in 1847, thus forming a large enclosed courtyard behind.

Immediately in front of the Palace, on an island surrounded by traffic, stands the Queen Victoria memorial, erected in 1911 as part of the memorial to the country's longest-reigning monarch.

Constitution Hill Now walk up Constitution Hill, so called, it has been suggested, because this was where Charles II took his constitutionals. No less than three attempts were made to assassinate Queen Victoria here during the 1840s. On the right-hand side lies Green Park, and on the left, behind the high wall, the 22 hectares (55 acres) of Buckingham Palace Gardens. Some 8,000 people are entertained at each of the three garden parties held there every summer.

Hyde Park Corner Use the pedestrian subway at the top of Constitution Hill to dive under the swirling traffic and re-emerge on the island in the middle of Hyde Park Corner. Constitution Arch was originally known as Wellington Arch, since a statue of Wellington once stood on top of it, but that is now replaced by a bronze chariot pulled by four horses with the figure of Peace. The sculptor served dinner for eight inside one of the horses shortly before finishing it. Inside the Arch is a tiny police station, the second smallest in London.

Wellington Museum This part of London belongs to the Duke of Wellington, the victor of Waterloo. At the far side of the island an equestrian statue of the Iron Duke astride his famous charger Copenhagen faces Apsley House, the Duke's London home, now reached via another set of subway passages. Wellington lived here from 1829 until his death in 1852. The house is now the Wellington Museum, stuffed full of paintings, medals, robes, uniforms, batons, porcelain and everything else imaginable, all associated with the Duke. It's a fascinating place to visit if you are interested in Wellington, somewhat overwhelming if you are not. Definitely worth a look, though, is the splendid 30-metre (90-foot) Waterloo Gallery, where the annual Waterloo Banquet was held every 18 June, attended by generals and other officers who had taken part in the battle. This room also contains the magnificent portrait by Goya of Wellington on horseback.

The walk finishes at the Museum.

Queen's Chapel

Marlborough Road
London SW1
Open to the public for morning service from 10.45 am each Sunday from Easter Day until the end of July.

Chapel Royal

Ambassadors Court
St James's Palace
London SW1
Open to the public for morning service from
10.45 am each Sunday from October to Good Friday.

Lancaster House
St James's Palace
London SW1
Opening times: April to October: Saturdays and
Sundays 2.00-4.00 pm when the building is not
required for government functions. Tel: 01-212 4784 to
check.

Royal Mews
Buckingham Palace
London SW1W 0QH
Tel: 01-930 4832 extension 634
Opening times: Wednesdays and Thursdays
2.00-4.00 pm; subject to occasional closures,
sometimes at short notice.

Wellington Museum
Apsley House
149 Piccadilly
Hyde Park Corner
London W1V 9FA
Tel: 01-499 5676
Opening times: Tuesdays, Wednesdays, Thursdays
and Saturdays 10.00 am-6.00 pm; Sundays
2.30-6.00 pm; closed Bank Holidays.

Changing Guard Ceremonies
Buckingham Palace
At 11.30 am daily from April to the end of July; on
alternate days from August to the end of March.
There is no Guard-changing in very wet weather,
and times may be changed on state occasions.
The Guards leave Wellington Barracks at 11.27 am
and march via Birdcage Walk to the palace.

St James's Palace
The St James's Palace Detachment of the Queen's Guard
leaves the palace at 11.15 am to march to Buckingham

Palace and returns at 12.10pm on days when the Guard is changed at Buckingham Palace.

Horse Guards, Whitehall
The Guard is changed at 11.00am Mondays to Saturdays and at 10.00am on Sundays throughout the year.
The Guard leaves Hyde Park Barracks at 10.28am (9.28am on Sundays) and rides via Hyde Park Corner and the Mall. Times may change on state occasions.

Tower of London
The Guard is changed at 11.30am on days when the Guard is changed at Buckingham Palace.

2   CORRIDORS OF POWER

Start: Clock Tower, Palace of Westminster
Underground: Westminster
Buses: 3, 11, 12, 24, 29, 53, 70, 76, 77, 77A, 88, 109, 159, 170, 184

Finish: Trafalgar Square
Underground: Charing Cross
Buses: 1, 1A, 3, 6, 9, 11, 12, 13, 15, 23, 24, 53, 77, 77A, 88, 159, 170, 173

Distance: 2·8 kilometres (1¾ miles)

Places to sit down: Victoria Tower Gardens, Millbank, St James's Park

Eating place: The Cake House, St James's Park

Lavatories: In pedestrian subway underneath end of Parliament Street. Opposite Central Hall

'Whitehall knows best' is the sarcastic catchphrase used to sum up the attitude of governments (of whatever political persuasion) that like to tell us what to do. This walk along and around Whitehall explores the favourite habitats of modern politicians and civil servants, and also recalls the days when this area was a royal palace.

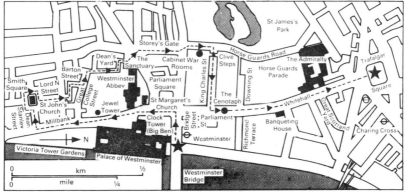

Big Ben   The walk begins on the south side of Bridge Street, by the exit from Westminster Underground Station and at what most people would describe as the foot of Big Ben. In fact, Big Ben is the name of the bell itself, not the clock tower. Big Ben was one of two people. According to one theory he was Sir Benjamin Hall, the portly Commissioner of Works at the time the bell was being named. Another version has it that he was Benjamin Caunt, a popular boxer (he weighed 114 kilogrammes, or 18 stones) who had recently gone to 60 rounds in a celebrated contest.

It is the first of Big Ben's chimes – which you can hear at the start of some BBC Radio news bulletins – that signifies the exact hour. The clock is claimed to be the most accurate public clock in the world, and its time is checked with the Royal Observatory at Greenwich (see walk 12) twice a day. It has four dials; the minute hands are 4.3 metres (14 feet) long and weigh more than 100 kilogrammes (2 cwt) each, and they travel about 160 kilometres (100 miles) a year; the hour hands are 2.7 metres (9 feet) long and each weighs over 300 kilogrammes (6 cwt). Big Ben itself only strikes the hours; it weighs 13½ tonnes and its hammer more than 200 kilogrammes (4 cwt). There are also four quarter bells.

Palace of Westminster There is a good view of the entire Palace of Westminster from the middle of Westminster Bridge. The palace includes the two Houses of Parliament: Commons and Lords. Broadly speaking, the Commons occupies that part of the Palace which is nearer to you as you stand on the bridge, the Lords the part further away. A long terrace, on which Members of Parliament and Peers (as members of the Commons and Lords are respectively known) like to entertain guests to tea or a drink, runs along the river embankment.

Although the Palace looks as though it dates from the Middle Ages, it was in fact built in the mid-19th century after a disastrous fire in 1834. The work took well over 20 years to complete. The original palace was a royal residence and, when the king was in London, the centre of the court from the time of Edward the Confessor – he was William the Conqueror's predecessor as king of England – until 1512, when Henry VIII moved to Whitehall Palace (see below). Officials worked here, and in Westminster Hall courts sat and the first Parliaments met. Civil courts continued to be held there until the late 19th century, when the Law Courts in the Strand were built (see walk 5).

New Palace Yard Walk down Bridge Street to the corner of Parliament Square, dominated by the statue of Sir Winston Churchill, and turn left. You are now passing New Palace Yard. This is the principal entrance for MPs, and when Parliament is sitting – usually from late October to late July, with breaks at Christmas, Easter and the end of May – there is always a hustle and bustle around the gates, with police stopping the traffic to let MPs' cars in and out.

Westminster Hall Beyond New Palace Yard is Westminster Hall, built in 1097 but altered several times since. It managed to survive both the fire in 1834 and the heavy bombing in the Second World War. Inside there is a magnificent hammerbeam roof, 28 metres (92 feet) high in the centre and the largest unsupported span in the country.

Old Palace Yard Next you pass St Stephen's Porch, the main public entrance to the House of Commons. Then comes Old Palace Yard, which is where Guy Fawkes and his co-

conspirators were executed in 1606 after they had been caught trying to blow up the Houses of Parliament the previous year. Every year before the State Opening of Parliament (see below), Yeomen of the Guard search the cellars of the Palace of Westminster in a ritual reenactment of that November night. Here, too, Sir Walter Raleigh was executed in 1618.

Opposite, sandwiched between the road and the massive bulk of Westminster Abbey, is the tiny church of St Margaret's, the parish church of the House of Commons. Winston Churchill married his Clementine here.

Jewel Tower A little way on is a small squat tower known as the Jewel Tower, the only surviving domestic part of the old Palace of Westminster. Inside there is a small exhibition on the history of Westminster with relics of the old palace – a contrast with the first 250 years of the building's life, from the mid-14th century onwards, when it held the monarch's jewels, gold, fur and clothes.

Victoria Tower Opposite is the Victoria Tower, 102 metres (336 feet) high and the world's tallest masonry tower. One of its functions is a document store, and it contains over 1½ million Acts of Parliament – every one, in fact, that has been passed since 1497.

Each autumn, when the Queen comes to Westminster to open the new session of Parliament, she enters by the Victoria Tower, and then climbs the Royal Staircase to the Robing Room. The Opening of Parliament takes place in the Chamber of the House of Lords, where the Queen reads the Queen's Speech to the assembled peers and MPs; the latter stand at the entrance to the Chamber. The Queen's Speech is not hers at all, but is written by senior civil servants on instructions from ministers, and contains details of the government's programme for the next year. When the monarch is present at Westminster, the Royal Standard flies from the Victoria Tower; the Union Jack is flown when Parliament is sitting. At night a light in the Clock Tower also shows that Parliament is still at work.

Now comes a short section of walk through some pleasant, small-scale streets, in which many of the houses remain private homes. MPs are among the residents here, as these streets are within reach of the division bell. When MPs vote after a debate (the technical term is a division), bells are rung throughout the House of Commons, and MPs have six minutes to reach the Division Lobby where they record their votes. Some of the houses here – and a few bars and restaurants as well – have division bells installed, and when a surprise vote is taken you can sometimes see MPs sprinting through the streets.

Smith Square Walk down Millbank – the Victoria Tower Gardens on the left are a good picnic spot – and turn right into Dean Stanley Street. In front of you as you enter Smith Square is St John's, a magnificent baroque church now used as a concert hall. A number of BBC chamber music recitals take place there. Smith Square is named after Henry Smith, who was the ground landlord when the square was built in about 1726. Walk clockwise around the square, past Transport House, the headquarters of the Transport and General Workers Union and until recently also of the Labour Party. (Its new headquarters are across the river near Elephant and Castle.) Almost immediately opposite is Conservative Central Office, the Conservative Party's headquarters.

Leave Smith Square by Lord North Street and turn left at the far end into Cowley Street. The offices of the Social Democratic Party are at number 4. A right turn at the end brings you into Barton Street, and then there is a left turn into Great College Street. Now go right through Dean's Yard. This is the heart of Westminster School, one of London's oldest and most distinguished public (i.e. not state-run) schools. At the far end, by the entrance to Westminster Abbey, you come out into The Sanctuary, so called because fugitives found sanctuary here from the forces of law.

Central Hall Cross the main road and continue up Storey's Gate, past Central Hall, which is the headquarters of the Methodist Church. Large public meetings are also held here, and in 1948 the United Nations Assembly met for the first time in Central Hall. Part of the building contains the Imperial

Collection, an exhibition of facsimile crown jewels and regalia from many countries.

At the top of Storey's Gate, turn left and immediately right into Horse Guards Road. St James's Park (see walk 1) is a magnificent picnic spot.

Now we really are in sight of the corridors of power. But it is hard to say who actually holds that power. Some people believe it is the politicians, the elected representatives of the people, and in particular the Cabinet, formed by the majority party in the House of Commons. Others – more cynically but more realistically – point to the power of civil servants, who are permanent fixtures, whereas politicians come and go every few years.

The Treasury The first block of government offices on the right contains the Treasury. The Treasury controls (or tries to control) how much money the Government spends, and decides on such things as how much we should pay in taxes. The people inside this building have more power to affect our daily lives than perhaps almost anyone else in Whitehall.

Cabinet War Rooms If the Treasury is the most important part of Whitehall today, the Cabinet War Rooms were undoubtedly the most important during the Second World War. The entrance is small and unobtrusive. Once underground, however, you enter a warren of corridors and bare cell-like rooms, now carefully restored to their wartime appearance. This was one of the main places where, in Britain at least, the war was planned and won. The War Cabinet met here more than a hundred times between 1940 and 1945. The Chiefs of Staff worked here, as did teams of planners and intelligence officers. Churchill himself had a room down here, although he rarely used it, preferring to sleep on the ground floor of the building above. One reason was the lack of lavatories underground!

Life was lived intensely down here. People worked under tremendous pressure, and the decisions taken here affected millions of lives. The lack of windows increases the sense of being cut off. People found out what the weather was like outside from a noticeboard in the main corridor.

Among many other rooms, all carefully restored to their

17

wartime appearance, you can see the cabinet room, with the large wooden chair from which Churchill presided, and the transatlantic telephone room, from which he spoke on a scrambled line to President Roosevelt in the USA. The offices have a rough and ready look about them – there was no time for smart decorations – with sometimes the human touch of a few family photographs. Often there is a camp bed tucked in the corner. The pace was so hectic down here that people often snatched just a few hours' sleep before getting back to work. The map room has large maps pinned to the wall, on which the progress of the fighting was plotted; the ones on display show the Russian front towards the end of the war in Germany.

The Cabinet War Rooms are well worth a visit. They give a real sense of the atmosphere of the Second World War, without any of the romanticism so often associated with it nowadays.

Outside again, walk up Clive Steps, past the statue of Robert Clive, who ran the East India Company for many years, and along King Charles Street. You can peer a little way into the elegant central court of the Foreign and Commonwealth Office on your left.

Downing Street At the end of King Charles Street turn left along Parliament Street. The next road on the left is Downing Street, which for security reasons is no longer open to pedestrians. The Prime Minister works at number 10, and also has a private flat on its upper floors. The Cabinet Room is on the ground floor. The Chancellor of the Exchequer, the minister responsible for the country's economy, uses number 11, and at number 12 is the Government Chief Whip. Although his job is not so well known, it is extremely important: to make sure that as many as possible of the Government's supporters in the House of Commons turn out to vote for its bills. A good Chief Whip keeps in close touch with ordinary MPs, and reports their views to the Prime Minister. He also attends Cabinet meetings.

Altogether, about 65 people work at number 10. From the front the house seems quite small, but it extends a long way back. Downing Street, or at least the terrace of which number 10 is part, was built by George Downing, who became Secretary of the Treasury at the end of the 17th century.

Whitehall   Going north up Whitehall, you pass the Cenotaph, erected in memory of the dead of the First World War. The annual Remembrance Day service, when those killed in both world wars are commemorated, is held there each November. On the left is the Cabinet Office and the Scottish Office, and on the right is Richmond Terrace, originally built in 1825 and now being restored, and the ugly huge mass of the Ministry of Defence, topped by its radio masts.

The only redeeming thing about the Ministry of Defence is that, quite unexpectedly, it has a wine cellar in its basement. The cellar belonged to Henry VIII, and is all that is left of York Palace, the London palace of the Archbishops of York, which later became Whitehall Palace (see below). When the Ministry was being built in the 1950s, the entire cellar, which weighs 1,000 tonnes and is 19 metres (66 feet) long, 10 metres (32 feet) wide and 6 metres (20 feet) high, had to be moved 5.7 metres (18 feet 9 inches).

Banqueting House   In front of the Ministry of Defence is the Banqueting House, a relatively modest building which is the sole survivor of Whitehall, the royal palace that has given its name to this stretch of the road between Trafalgar Square and Parliament Square. It was Henry VIII who, having got tired of the Palace of Westminster, confiscated York Palace from Cardinal Wolsey, and renamed and extended it. The palace was the focus of a glittering court life for the best part of two centuries (except for the period of the Commonwealth, when Oliver Cromwell was in power), until the dual monarchs William and Mary came to the throne. They preferred to live in relative peace at Kensington Palace (see walk 3) and transferred their private residence there. Ten years later, in 1698, Whitehall Palace was gutted by fire.

The only building to escape that disastrous fire was the Banqueting House, completed in 1622 by the architect Inigo Jones. Apart from the mere fact of having survived, the building is notable for two things. The saloon, which is a double cube measuring 34 metres by 17 by 17 (110 feet by 55 by 55), has a magnificent ceiling by the Flemish artist Peter Paul Rubens. And it was from a window in the Banqueting House, probably the one above the present entrance, that one January day in 1649 King Charles I stepped out on to the scaffold.

Horse Guards

Opposite the Banqueting House is Horse Guards. The first building on this site was simply a small guardhouse for Whitehall Palace. Nowadays guard is mounted daily between 10.00 am and 4.00 pm by troops of the Royal Household Cavalry, either the Life Guards in their red tunics and white plumes or the Royal Horse Guards in their blue tunics and red plumes. Each trooper is on duty for an hour at a time. The Guard is changed daily at 11.00 am (10.00 am on Sundays).

Horse Guards Parade

Beyond the arch, through which only members of the royal family may ride, you come to Horse Guards Parade, a wide stretch of open ground normally used as a car park for civil servants. In the days of Whitehall Palace this was a tilt-yard where jousts and tournaments were held. In modern times the annual Trooping the Colour ceremony takes place here every June. This is a magnificent spectacle at which the Queen takes the salute on horseback (she has to ride side-saddle, even though she prefers to ride astride) as one battalion from one of the five regiments of Foot Guard troops its colours, that is, parades the battalion flags and banners.

The walk continues up Whitehall past Admiralty House and the Admiralty on the left. Down Whitehall Place on the right is the National Liberal Club, which houses the headquarters of the Liberal Party. Great Scotland Yard, also on the right, is famous as the first headquarters of the Metropolitan Police, established in 1829. The name dates back much further, for a house here belonged to the kings of Scotland as long ago as the 10th century.

The walk finishes at Trafalgar Square.

Jewel Tower

Old Palace Yard
Westminster
London SW1
Tel: 01-222 2219
Opening times: 15 March to 15 October: daily except
Sundays 9.30 am-6.00 pm; 16 October to 14 March: daily
except Sundays 9.30 am-4.00 pm
NB The Jewel Tower is often closed at short notice, and
always closes for lunch between 1.00 and 2.00 pm

Palace of Westminster

The Palace of Westminster, Westminster Hall and the
Clock Tower are not open to the public. The public may,
however, attend debates in the House of Commons and
the House of Lords. The only way to be sure of getting
a seat for the Strangers' Gallery in either House is to ask
your MP for seats well in advance: each MP has a small
allocation of tickets each year. Alternatively you can queue
for seats outside the St Stephen's entrance. Admission
to the Commons is from 4.15 pm on Mondays to
Thursdays and from 10.00 am on Fridays; to the Lords
from 2.40 pm on Tuesdays to Thursdays and on some
Mondays. But be aware that you may have a long wait, and
on days when an important debate is being held you may
not get in at all.

Further information about the work of the House of
Commons can be obtained from:
The Public Information Office
House of Commons
London SW1
Tel: 01-219 4272

Information about the House of Lords is available
from:
Journal and Information Office
House of Lords
London SW1
Tel: 01-219 3107

Imperial Collection

Central Hall
Westminster
London SW1
Tel: 01-222 0770
Opening times: April to October: daily except Sundays
10.00-6.00pm; November to March: daily except Sundays
11.00am-5.00pm; last admission 45 minutes before
closing time

Cabinet War Rooms

Clive Steps
King Charles Street
London SW1A 2AQ
Tel: 01-930 6961
Opening times: Tuesdays to Sundays 10.00am-5.50pm;
last admission 5.15pm; open some Bank Holidays

The Henry VIII Wine Cellar

Whitehall
London SW1
Opening times: April to September: Saturdays 2.30-
4.30pm. Advance booking required. Contact:
Property Services Agency
Room 10/14
St Christopher House
Southwark Street
London SE1 0TE
Tel: 01-921 4849
The way in is at the north entrance to the Ministry of
Defence, Horse Guards Avenue

Banqueting House

Whitehall
London SW1
Tel: 01-930 4179
Opening times: Tuesdays to Saturdays
10.00am-5.00pm; Sundays 2.00-5.00pm;
closed some Bank Holidays, and also sometimes at
short notice for government functions

3   TWO ROYAL PARKS

Start: Speakers' Corner
Underground: Marble Arch
Buses: 2, 2B, 6, 7, 8, 12, 15, 16, 16A, 23, 25, 30, 36, 36B, 73, 74, 88, 137, 500

Finish: Marlborough Gate, Bayswater Road
Underground: Lancaster Gate
Buses: 12, 88
or
Finish: Black Lion Gate, Bayswater Road
Underground: Queensway
Buses: 12, 88
or
Finish: Speakers' Corner, as above

Distance: 6·5 kilometres (4 miles)

Eating-place: Café by Serpentine Bridge

Lavatories: In parks, as shown on display maps

A broad swathe of green runs across central London, giving Londoners the chance to escape in what with a little imagination can almost seem like country. This route is a meander through two royal parks: Hyde Park and Kensington Gardens. If you feel like a rest from sightseeing, you could hardly do better than spend a day here. Between them the two parks offer a wide variety of things to do and see and, as everywhere in London, there is the added bonus of watching Londoners themselves.

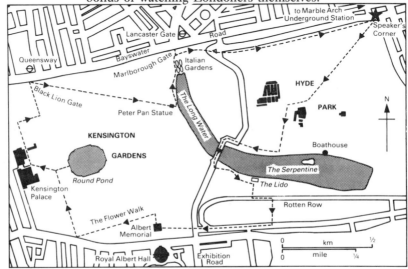

Marble Arch The walk begins in one of London's least attractive spots, both now and in the past. Today, it is traffic – streams and streams of it, rushing past 24 hours a day – that makes Marble Arch almost unbearable. In the past it was something far more sinister: the gallows.

The Arch is a relatively new arrival here. It was erected on its present site in 1851, having stood in front of Buckingham Palace for 24 years before that. Its design is a copy of an ancient Roman arch. The gates within it are almost permanently closed, for the only people allowed to ride through are senior members of the Royal Family and the King's Troop Royal Horse Artillery.

The gallows were those of Tyburn. Thousands of people met their death here – thieves, murderers, pickpockets, sheepstealers, religious martyrs among them –

having made the grisly final journey from Newgate Prison (see walk 9). They received a nosegay of flowers and a last mug of ale *en route*. Execution days were public holidays, and huge crowds of people flocked to see the executions; no less than 200,000 came one day in 1714 to see Jack Sheppard die. He was a notorious thief who had escaped from prison many times. The proceedings of Tyburn were something of a production line, for the triangular gallows could accommodate up to 24 victims at a time.

Speakers' Corner Of all this grimness there is now no sign, and the walk is best begun in the north-east corner of Hyde Park, at Speakers' Corner. (If you do want to examine the Arch in detail, take exits 3 or 10 from the warren of subways underneath the road junction.) Every Sunday morning orators set up their soapboxes and give forth their views. Come here, and you will hear religious, social and political views of almost every persuasion – and, it can almost be guaranteed, of some persuasions you never imagined existed. It's all free. Anyone may say anything, so long as it's not obscene or blasphemous and isn't a breach of the peace, or likely to cause one. Anyone may heckle (the best hecklers are at least as entertaining as the speakers they are interrupting), and there is nothing to stop you getting up on your feet if you want to.

Hyde Park Strike south-west across the park, heading towards the distant clump of wood and following signs towards the Serpentine Lido. (There is a refreshment kiosk a little way down the path parallel to Park Lane.) This part of the park is quite open, and is often used as the starting- or finishing-point of marches and demonstrations. It was just such occasions in the mid-19th century that led to the creation of Speakers' Corner in 1872; before then there was no legal right of assembly.

Hyde Park is the largest of the five royal parks in central London. Henry VIII was the monarch who got his hands on the land – it had belonged previously to a monastery – and turned it into a hunting-ground. Hunting continued here for the next 200 years or so, although the public was admitted early in the 17th century. The park became a place for duels, which are no longer held, and for national celebrations, which are. George IV's coronation was fêted here in 1820 with fireworks, and 161 years later the marriage of Prince Charles and Lady Diana Spencer was similarly celebrated. On the former occasion – but not on the latter – elephants were part of the spectacle.

Having reached the trees, take the path just north of the police station. Each royal park has its own police force – except for Hyde Park, which is patrolled by the Metropolitan Police. The station here has about 36 officers and constables during the summer, and rather fewer in winter.

The path passes the entrance to several hectares of greenhouses, where the park's gardeners cultivate plants for all the royal parks, and then the memorial to W.H. Hudson, the naturalist and writer. Both Hyde Park and Kensington Gardens are a haven for birds, with almost 100 species recorded. Cormorants have been seen fishing in the Serpentine, and herons and little grebe on Long Water.

The Serpentine Now turn south and make for the Serpentine, formed in 1730 by damming the Westbourne river. Rowing on the Serpentine is one of *the* traditional things to do in London, and, unlike many traditions, it is still worth doing. Boats can be hired near the east end of the lake, on the north bank.

The walk passes across the Serpentine Bridge. Confusingly, although it is a single stretch of water, that part of the lake south-east of the bridge is known as the Serpentine, and the part to the north-west as Long Water. Immediately beyond the bridge is a group of restaurants, one of which serves fairly cheap drinks and snacks. (There is also a restaurant at the east end of the lake, beyond the Boat House.) The views from the bridge are splendid, especially east towards the Houses of Parliament and Whitehall.

The Lido Past the restaurants, on the southern shore of the Serpentine, you come to the Lido, where you can laze and swim in the sun. Contrary to myth, London is a sunny place; on an average June day there are nearly seven hours of sunshine. In hard winters, skating on the Serpentine is sometimes possible.

Rotten Row   A few steps south towards the edge of the park bring you to Rotten Row – about which there is nothing rotten at all. Quite the contrary: it is one of London's most fashionable places to go riding. The name derives from *Route du roi* – literally, 'the King's Way' – the king being William III, who built the road to link Kensington Palace, where he and his co-monarch Mary lived (see below), and the West End. Rotten Row had 300 lamps hung from the branches of trees, thus becoming the first road with street lighting in England, and it soon became the place for people of fashion to promenade.

In 1851 this part of the park was taken over by the Great Exhibition, a fabulous celebration of British achievement in the arts, crafts and sciences. The exhibits, which were seen by more than 6 million visitors, were displayed in a huge glass building, the famous Crystal Palace. Of the Exhibition nothing now remains (the Crystal Palace was dismantled and re-erected at Sydenham in south London) except the Coalbrookdale Gates and the name Exhibition Road given to the main approach to this part of the park. Some of the proceeds from the Great Exhibition went towards setting up the South Kensington Arts Centre, out of which developed the different South Kensington museums. These museums – the Victoria and Albert, the Natural History, the Geological and the Science – are all a short walk down Exhibition Road. Each is packed full of interesting things and deserves as long a visit as you can manage.

Albert Memorial   Our path continues west through the Park, past the Coalbrookdale Gates (at the junction of Prince of Wales' Gate and the north-south road across Hyde Park) and along to the Albert Memorial. This has been one of London's most derided monuments, some people wondering when the spaceship is to be launched. Opinions differ: my own is that it is a magnificent example of Victorian grandeur. Albert, who married Queen Victoria in 1840, was one of the principal organizers of the Great Exhibition and is portrayed holding an Exhibition catalogue. Opposite is the Royal Albert Hall, also named in memory of the Prince.

Kensington Gardens We are now in Kensington Gardens. Although this park was part of the land acquired by Henry VIII, it remained private for far longer, and was only opened to the public in the 19th century, after Queen Victoria had moved to Buckingham Palace. Even then visitors had to be respectably dressed – a condition that does not apply nowadays! These gardens seem much more exclusive than Hyde Park. You might see a nanny out for a walk with her charge, or a group of children from one of the smart preparatory schools nearby.

Kensington Palace Turn west now along the Flower Walk, carefully planted so that there are flowers in bloom almost throughout the year, and then strike across the park to the Round Pond, where enthusiasts of all ages congregate to sail their model boats and ships. West of the pond is a statue of Queen Victoria, aptly positioned in front of Kensington Palace, her childhood home and the place where, one early morning in 1837, when she was just 18, she learnt that she had become Queen.

The house itself looks more like a country house than a royal palace – which indeed it was before William and Mary bought it in 1689. Appearances are deceptive, however. Modest though the exterior may seem, the State Apartments inside are splendid, mainly the result of alterations in the early 18th century. There are splendid ceilings and carvings, and a magnificent Grand Staircase, with wall paintings beside it from which contemporary members of the royal court look out. In Queen Victoria's bedroom you can see the cot in which each of Victoria's nine offspring slept. Downstairs there is a fascinating exhibition of court dress over the last 200 years.

Most of the palace is still very much a royal residence. Princess Margaret lives here, as do Prince and Princess Michael of Kent, and the Prince and Princess of Wales, Alice, Dowager Duchess of Gloucester, and the Duke and Duchess of Gloucester all have their London homes here. Naturally, there is no public admission to these parts of the building.

Kensington Palace Gardens Walk through the lovely palace gardens – the sunken garden is especially attractive – north towards the Orangery. Oranges are no longer grown here, but especially in hot weather it is a deliciously cool building, with plants and benches and statues. North from here is a children's playground and the stump of an oak tree, known as the Elfin Oak, full of gnomes, fairies and little animals. The oak was first placed here in 1930 and has recently been restored by the comic actor Spike Milligan.

You could leave the gardens here through Black Lion Gate for Notting Hill and Bayswater, where there are interesting shops and some lively eating-places, and also the famous Portobello Road market. The Queen's Ice Club is a little way down Queensway.

Peter Pan Our walk continues roughly south-east across the gardens in the general direction of the Long Water. Soon you will reach an obelisk in memory of John Hanning Speke, a celebrated Victorian explorer who discovered the source of the Nile. A little way on, by the water's edge, is what must be London's most celebrated statue: Peter Pan, the little boy who never grew up, playing his pipes. Sir James Barrie, the author, was living not far away at number 100 Bayswater Terrace when he created Peter. On the opposite bank is a piece of work 5.8 metres (19 feet) high by the British sculptor Henry Moore called *The Arch*.

Follow the water round to the Italian Gardens, where there are fountains and seats amid the formal flower beds. You can either finish the walk here at Marlborough Gate (Lancaster Gate Underground Station is on the opposite side of the main road) or continue along the north side of Hyde Park, past a children's playground and so to Marble Arch.

Serpentine Boats

Opening times: 1 March to 30 September: daily from 10.00 am; 1 October to 28 February: Saturdays and Sundays from 10.00 am

Serpentine Lido

Tel: 01-262 5484
Opening times: Mid-May to mid-September: daily
6.00 am-7.00 pm; mid-September to mid-May: daily
6.00-10.00 am
The Lido closes at 2.00 pm in summer if no swimmers are
present and more are unlikely to arrive.

Kensington Palace

The Broad Walk
Kensington Gardens
London W8
Tel: 01-937 9561
Opening times: Mondays to Saturdays 9.00 am-5.00 pm;
Sundays 1.00-5.00 pm; last tickets sold 45 minutes
before closing time; closed some Bank Holidays

4   IN AND AROUND THE GARDEN

Start: Trafalgar Square
Underground: Charing Cross
Buses: 1, 1A, 3, 6, 9, 11, 12, 13, 15, 23, 24, 53, 77, 77A, 88, 159, 170, 173

Finish: Central Market, Covent Garden
Underground: Covent Garden
Buses: 1, 1A, 4, 5, 6, 9, 11, 13, 15, 23, 68, 77, 77A, 155, 170, 171, 176, 188, 501, 502, 513

Distance: 3·4 kilometres (2 miles)

Places to sit down: Victoria Embankment Gardens Churchyard, St Paul's, Covent Gardens

Eating places: Food for Thought, Neal Street
Neal's Yard
Cranks, Central Market,
Covent Garden

Lavatories: On the Embankment, just east of
Embankment Underground Station
On the west side of Central Market,
Covent Garden

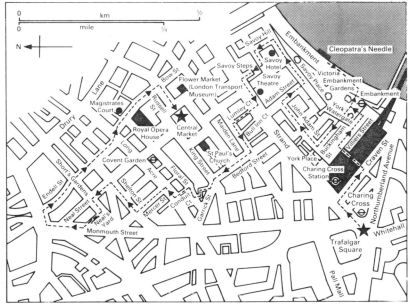

London draws much of its fascination from the variety and individuality of different, quite small blocks of streets. Walk just a kilometre in central London, and not much more than that in the Victorian inner suburbs, and you are guaranteed to experience a complete change of environment and atmosphere.

This route starts at Trafalgar Square, the official centre of London, and passes through two quite distinct areas: the group of 18th-century streets around the Adelphi, and Covent Garden. It also demonstrates the radical effect – sometimes good, more often positively harmful – that rebuilding and modernization schemes can have on the environment of the capital.

Trafalgar Square The junction of three main thoroughfares – Whitehall, Pall Mall and the Strand – was an important one for centuries. Trafalgar Square itself is a relatively new arrival. It was created during the 1830s by John Nash (see also walks 2, 9 and 10), although he died before it was finished. Nelson, the victor of the Battle of Trafalgar against France, was placed 49 metres (162 feet) on top of his column in 1843, the fountains and basins were installed a couple of years later, and the four Landseer lions (each 6 metres long by 6½ metres wide, or 20 feet by 22) that guard the base of the column took up their positions as late as 1867.

Trafalgar Square can be a disappointing place, untidy and crowded with tourists, pigeons and pigeon-droppings, although the pigeons never fail to entrance young children. There are, though, plenty of magical moments: at 10 o'clock in the morning, when the fountains start to play; in the two weeks before Christmas, when Londoners gather to sing carols underneath the huge Christmas tree given each year by the people of Norway; and on New Year's Eve, when crowds gather to greet the new year.

Towards the base of the inside of the north wall of the square (the National Gallery side) is a set of imperial measurements, showing definitive 1-foot, 2-foot and 1-yard lengths. Within the wall at the south-east corner is a minute police station, used when crowds gather in the square for rallies and demonstrations. It has a direct phone link with New Scotland Yard.

London's Centre To begin the walk, cross over the end of the Strand, turn left up it a little way and then turn right into Craven Street, where Benjamin Franklin, the American ambassador, inventor and man of letters, lived for 13 years. On the corner of the Strand and Northumberland Avenue, by Vines' camera shop, a plaque marks the exact centre of London. All distances to London given on road signs refer to this point.

From Craven Street turn left along The Arches running under the railway lines that lead into Charing Cross Station, and then go right into Villiers Street. The streets around here were built following the demolition of a grand mansion known as York House in 1670. York House had belonged to George Villiers, Duke of Buckingham, and every word of his title was commemorated in the streets around here – even the 'of', although sadly Of Alley has now been renamed York Place.

On the right is the Players' Theatre, where old-time music hall shows are given. Turn left into Victoria Embankment Gardens where there is a small tea place optimistically named the Paradise Café, and cross the Embankment.

Victoria Embankment

Until just over 100 years ago, the spot on which you are now standing was under several metres of muddy Thames water. The Strand – the word simply means 'shore' – used to be the main Thameside thoroughfare, with small side streets leading to the water's edge. Proposals to construct a riverside road from the City to Westminster had been discussed for two centuries. But work only started in the 1860s. Not only was a new road built, but the tracks of the District Line Underground were also laid underneath it, and pipes for London's new sewage system. No less than 15 hectares (37 acres) were reclaimed, and in some spots the width of the river was reduced by as much as 30 metres (100 feet).

Cleopatra's Needle

A little way along the Embankment stands Cleopatra's Needle, an ancient Egyptian obelisk now well over 3,500 years old and brought to Britain in 1878 – not without incident, for it was almost lost in a storm in the Bay of Biscay. Buried in the foundations are some day-to-day items of contemporary interest, including a set of morning newspapers and another of coins, four Bibles, a Bradshaw (the complete railway timetable of Britain), a razor, a box of pins, and photographs of 12 of the most attractive ladies of the day. Who chose this curious assortment of relics, and in particular who picked out the 12 lucky ladies, history does not relate.

Adelphi

Now re-cross the gardens towards York Watergate. The Watergate, as the name implies, was the river entrance to York House, and is all that remains of the palace. Walk up Buckingham Street, where some pleasant old houses survive (number 11 has some good gargoyles), and turn right at the top into John Adam Street. Here the Adam brothers (there were four of them: James, John, Robert and William) built the Adelphi in the 1770s. The word *adelphoi* is Greek for 'brothers'.

Nowadays the Adelphi would be described as a luxury riverside development. Eleven sumptuously decorated houses along the Royal Terrace faced the river, and there were several streets with similar houses behind. The project almost ruined the Adam brothers, and a lottery was organized to enable them to complete it.

Virtually nothing remains of their work. At number 8 the Royal Society of Arts occupies the house the brothers built for the Society; the interior is splendid, but unfortunately not open to the public. Number 7 Adam Street, just at the end of John Adam Street, is another attractive survivor. The *Lancet*, the well-known medical journal, has its offices here. There is a massive new block on the Adelphi site which makes some effort to recapture the elegance of the original, but with little success.

Savoy Place   From John Adam Street, turn right into Adam Street and then left down the steps into the end of Savoy Place. Here for over 500 years until the early 19th century stood Savoy Palace. At first it was a ducal residence. Then, for many centuries, it was used as a hospital for the poor. The connection with Savoy, a region in south-eastern France, came about because, even before the palace was built, Henry III rented the land to the Count of Savoy.

Savoy Hotel   A palace of a different kind occupies the site now: the Savoy Hotel, built in the 1880s by Richard D'Oyly Carte, who had made his money staging the Gilbert and Sullivan operas. When it opened the hotel was the last word in luxury – and it retains that reputation today. The original hotel generated its own electricity supply and possessed its own artesian well; each room was equipped with speaking tubes, the early version of the telephone; and – a quite novel feature – ascending rooms conducted guests to their rooms. Two of the original ascending rooms – or lifts, as we call them now – are still in use today. Celebrities from every walk of life – royalty, statesmen and politicians, million-aires, show business people – have all stayed at the Savoy.

Walk past the entrance to the hotel and turn left up Savoy Hill. From the Institute of Electrical Engineers building on the left, just beyond the junction with Savoy Hill, the BBC (the initials then stood for British Broadcasting Company, not Corporation as they do now), the first national radio station in the world, made its first broadcast in 1923. Its famous call-sign was '2LO'. Just beyond the IEE, on the Embankment, is a rarity: a telephone box painted green instead of the usual red.

From Savoy Hill, turn left into Savoy Way and then immediately right up the steps of the Savoy Buildings. The passage leads directly underneath the hotel. Look up to the windows high above and you may see chefs at work (and even, as I once did – horror of horrors! – a sauce bottle).

Savoy Steps lead into the Strand. Immediately on the left is the other main entrance to the Savoy. Traffic drives on the right here – the only place in the UK where this is allowed. The reason? To enable theatre-goers attending the Savoy Theatre to alight from their carriages easily. Permission had to be granted in a special Act of Parliament.

Now cross the Strand and turn right up Bull Inn Court or Lumley Court, both of which finish in Maiden Lane. This is the southern edge of Covent Garden.

Covent Garden The word Covent comes from Convent. In the Middle Ages the land here was the kitchen garden of a monastery attached to Westminster Abbey, where fruit and vegetables were grown for the monks. The land passed into the ownership of the Earls of Bedford, and the Bedfords, who later became dukes, continued to own it until the early 20th century. In the early 1630s the 3rd Earl commissioned a new development scheme from a fashionable architect called Inigo Jones, who was much influenced by contemporary Italian buildings. Inigo Jones produced London's first square. On one side was a church, St Paul's, which has survived, on the other three there were smart town houses opening into arcades, which have not.

The project was not a great success, and Covent Garden did not long remain a fashionable address. As early as the 1670s a market was operating in the square. The area gradually went downhill, and the upperclass residents moved out. By the early 19th century all kinds of goods as well as fruit and vegetables were being sold.

The first market building was erected in 1830. Almost immediately people started to grumble about overcrowding, and the grumbles continued for the next 130 years, despite the construction of three more market buildings: the Floral Hall, the Flower Market and the Jubilee Hall. Every working day the narrow streets were jammed with vehicles bringing produce from all over the country. It was all very atmospheric – and very inefficient. Finally, the decision was taken about 20 years ago to move the wholesale market to a new site south of the river at Nine Elms in Battersea, which opened in 1974.

One result of this decision was a major battle about the future of the area. It was an unusual battle, for it was not just a dispute about one of the only parts of central London that had escaped being comprehensively redeveloped and scattered with office blocks during the previous century. It was also a struggle for the survival of a genuinely local community: a village of about 2,000 people, young and old, in the heart of London.

On one side were the property developers and the council, who put forward a scheme for massive redevelopment, with a jungle of massive office blocks and a conference centre, a motorway, and just a few, expensive, houses and flats. On the other side was almost everyone else: local residents, ordinary Londoners, conservationists.

In the end, after noisy meetings, colourful demonstrations and a lot of publicity, the property developers lost, and their plans were thrown out. Since the mid-1970s Covent Garden has continued to change and improve, but gradually and usually with considerable sensitivity. The old buildings probably look smarter now than they ever have, and many of the tenement flats have been modernized and given bathrooms. New homes have been built, many of them council houses and flats that ordinary working people can afford. The central Market Building has been restored, and work is under way on the others (see below). The population too has increased. In 1981 about 4,000 people lived in Covent Garden, and at long last young children are growing up here; the local primary schools are full to bursting.

Nowadays Covent Garden is an exciting place to visit. There are fascinating shops, a variety of places to eat, museums, dance studios, market halls, and the added bonus of free high-quality street entertainment every day. For residents it is certainly far better than it would have been if the developers had won. However, living in the middle of an extremely popular tourist spot does have its disadvantages: land is expensive and rents are high, so that ordinary shops – grocers, ironmongers, butchers – which people use every day find it difficult to make a living. Until recently there was no doctor's surgery. There are no open spaces, and one of the Garden's more ugly and unfriendly office blocks was built on the site of the old community garden, on the corner of Endell Street and Long Acre.

The best way to enjoy Covent Garden is simply to stroll around and look at whatever takes your fancy. The central market area is a must, of course. But do try to explore further afield. The streets north of Long Acre, for instance, preserve some of the old Covent Garden atmosphere.

St Paul's Church The route that follows is just one suggestion for a walk. From Bull Inn or Lumley Court, turn left along Maiden Lane and then right up Bedford Street. The entrance to St Paul's Church is on the right, and there are pleasant seats in the churchyard. This is the actors' church. Covent Garden has always had close links with the theatre; many actors have lived in the area; and two of London's biggest and best-known theatres, the Royal Opera House and the Theatre Royal, Drury Lane, are not far away.

London Stamp Centre On the corner of Bedford Street and King Street is the London Stamp Centre, an indoor market where a number of stamp-dealers occupy small shops. You can browse here freely.

Go left along Garrick Street and then immediately right along Rose Street and through the passage by the Lamb and Flag pub. Next it is right into Floral Street, left into Conduit Court and right into Long Acre, just opposite the site where John Logie Baird broadcast the first television programme in Great Britain, on 30 September 1929. Turn left into Mercer Street and right along Shelton Street.

(Take care here as the pavements are extremely narrow.) Some of the old warehouses here have been converted into studios and small offices.

Neal Street Take another turn left, into Neal Street. There are excellent shops here. Neal Street East, a little way down Neal Street in the other direction, is full of goods from the Far East, many at quite reasonable prices. There is a well-stocked postcard gallery, and Food for Thought is an interesting and fairly cheap place to eat. A turn left into Short's Gardens and then right brings you into Neal's Yard, a fascinating corner where you can buy and eat delicious wholefood snacks, as well as fruit, dairy produce and cereals.

At the far end of Neal's Yard turn right into Monmouth Street, right again at the crossroads, and right for a third time into Endell Street. The Oasis on the corner of Endell Street is well named. Here there is an indoor and an outdoor swimming-pool – where else can you swim outdoors slap-bang in the middle of London? – and ordinary public baths as well. These are used by local residents, for a few of the older flats nearby are still without bathrooms.

Walk down Endell Street. The Covent Garden Community Association just round the corner at number 4 Short's Gardens has details of local community events. It led the fight to save the area in the 1970s, a battle commemorated by the mural on the fish and chip shop in Endell Street.

London Ecology Centre A little way further down Endell Street, just round the corner in Shelton Street, you reach the London Ecology Centre. This is just the kind of organization that would have been shut out of the brave new Covent Garden which was planned in the early 1970s. The Centre has a coffee shop, an Ecology Shop, and an interesting variety of exhibitions on ecology and conservation.

The streets around here are some of the most residential in the Garden. Look up and you will see net curtains, window boxes and all the signs of domestic life.

Bow Street   Continue to the end of Endell Street and carry straight on into Bow Street, so called because it was built in the shape of a bow. The Royal Opera House is on the right, the Magistrate's Court on the left. The Bow Street Runners, a semi-official group of foot patrols who were the London's first policemen, were founded here in the mid-18th century. They were only disbanded in 1839 after the Metropolitan Police had been formed.

Covent Garden Market   The end of the walk is at the market, reached by turning right along Russell Street off Bow Street. In front of you is the central market building with five avenues and a basement full of intriguing shops and restaurants (Cranks is especially recommended). At Light Fantastic in South Row there is an amazing exhibition of holograms. A craft market is held in the Apple Market outside the market building at weekends, and the Jubilee Hall houses a sports centre. The Jubilee Market (which has 'ordinary' market stalls on four days a week and craft stalls on the other days) is currently being redeveloped by a consortium that includes many local interests, and will provide a market area, more sports facilities, cheap housing and a few offices. A national Theatre Museum will open in the basement of the Flower Market, the rest of which is already occupied by the London Transport Museum.

London Transport Museum   The London Transport Museum provides an exceptionally interesting view of the history of transport in London and of the way it operates today. It is a 'hands-on' Museum, with real equipment you can handle yourself – try turning the steering wheel of a modern bus, for instance, or operating computerized bus control equipment. A large number of trams and buses (both horse-drawn and motorized) are on display, together with Underground rolling stock. Display panels and showcases (with many of the more interesting objects at child's-eye level) fill you in on the detailed history. (Did you know, for instance, that the earliest buses were hailed much as taxis are today?) A good range of activity sheets is on sale.

The Oasis
32 Endell Street
London WC2
Tel: 01-836 3771
Opening times: Indoor pool Mondays to Fridays
9.00 am-6.45 pm; Saturdays 9.00 am-4.45 pm;
Sundays 9.00 am-5.45 pm
Outdoor pool Mondays to Fridays 9.00 am-7.45 pm

London Ecology Centre
45 Shelton Street
Covent Garden
London WC2H 9HJ
Tel: 01-379 4324
Opening times: normally Mondays to Fridays and
some Saturdays 10.00 am-6.00 pm

Light Fantastic Gallery of Holography
48 South Row
The Market
Covent Garden
London WC2E 8I IN
Tel: 01-836 6423; 01-836 6424
Opening times: Sundays to Wednesdays
10.00 am-6.00 pm; Thursdays and Fridays
10.00 am-8.00 pm; Saturdays 10.00 am-7.00 pm

London Transport Museum
Covent Garden
London WC2E 7BB
Tel: 01-379 6344
Opening times: daily 10.00 am-6.00 pm; last
admission 5.15 pm

5   WIG AND PEN

Start: Temple Underground Station, Embankment
Buses: 1, 1A, 4, 5, 6, 9, 11, 13, 15, 23, 68, 77, 77A,
155, 170, 171, 172, 176, 188, 501, 502, 513
(all at Aldwych)

Finish: Kingsway
Underground: Holborn
Buses: As above, at Aldwych

Distance: 3.6 kilometres (2¼ miles)

Places to sit down: Fountain Court, Middle Temple
St Bride's Churchyard Gardens,
Lincoln's Inn (Mondays to
Fridays 12.00-2.30 pm)

Eating places: Food for Health, Blackfriars Lane
Chubbies Sandwich Bar,
89 Fleet Street
Tea bar, Lincoln's Inn Fields

Lavatories: In centre of the Strand, east of
St Clement Dane's Church

All the world knows that Fleet Street is the centre of
British newspaper life. Most journalists aspire to a job on
'The Street', and some still dream of a world scoop that
will lead to fame and fortune. Even today, although a good
half of the national dailies have moved their offices away
from the immediate area, something of the old romance
remains. The sense of urgency and excitement is almost
palpable – no more so than in the late evening, when the
presses thunder and the queues of delivery vans wait,
engines revving, to rush the first edition on to the streets.

Not so many people realize, however, that cheek by jowl
with Fleet Street is the centre of another traditional

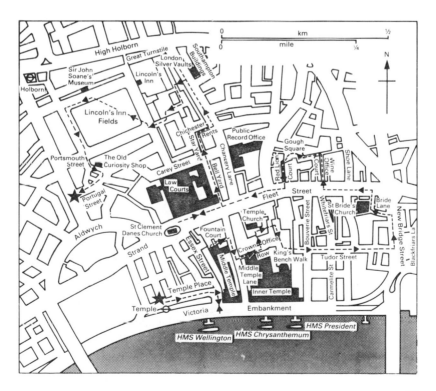

cornerstone of English society: the Law. The four Inns of Court conceal themselves in squares and courtyards and tiny passages that create an atmosphere of unhurried seclusion.

This walk explores the very different domains of the Law and the Press. The start is at Temple Underground Station.

Victoria Embankment
Turn right as you leave the station and cross the Embankment to the riverside. The three vessels moored here are *HMS Wellington, HMS Chrysanthemum* and *HMS President* (see walk 11 for further information). The grand stone arch, with the face of a bearded man at its apex, leads to Temple Pier and commemorates the naming of King's Reach – that stretch of the river between London Bridge and Westminster Bridge – on the occasion of George V's Silver Jubilee in 1935. Two dragons, one on each side of the road, mark the border between Westminster and the City of London; until the early 1960s they stood guard at the entrance to the now demolished City of London Coal Exchange. A plaque records Queen Victoria's last visit to the City in 1900, less than a year before she died.

Inns of Court
After this brief watery prelude (the view up and down the Thames is always worth a few minutes' time) the exploration of the Inns of Court begins in earnest. Originally, in the Middle Ages, the Inns of Court were places – legal universities almost – where lawyers lived and worked and dined and where students came to study their books and listen to lectures. Each of the Inns built working and living accommodation, a dininghall, a library and a chapel, and became almost a self-sufficient community, with its own rules and traditions.

Even in today's very different world, the Inns of Court hold on to many of their original functions. They are still responsible for much legal training. If you want to practise as a barrister anywhere in England or Wales you must be called to the Bar by one of the four Inns. As you would expect, this involves passing examinations. It also involves, as you might not so readily expect, eating meals: three dinners each term, to be precise, in the Hall of your Inn – an interesting link with the Inns' earliest history. Barristers and solicitors, including some of the country's most successful and sought after practitioners of the law, have chambers in the Inns of Court, and a few even live here as well.

Middle Temple   Re-cross the Embankment, walk a few yards up Temple Place and then turn into Middle Temple through a small gate. Two of the four Inns of Court, Middle Temple and Inner Temple, occupy the area generally known as Temple, so called because the Knights Templar owned land there from the 12th century. There is no clear division on the ground between the two Temples. Turn left inside the gate, and walk through Garden Court, up the steps and into Fountain Court.

If you find the gate into Middle Temple closed, as you may well do at weekends, walk up Essex Street, turn right at the top into the Strand, which becomes Fleet Street, and then enter the Temple through either Middle Temple or Inner Temple Gateway.

Fountain Court is typical of the quiet courts and passages of the Temple, whose atmosphere is best absorbed by wandering round for half an hour or so. During the week there can be something of a bustle, especially when the Law Courts on the far side of the Strand (see below) rise at 4.00 pm and the lawyers come streaming back to their chambers. At weekends, by contrast, the calm is rarely disturbed.

The chambers and their inhabitants are easy enough to spot from the list of names painted on the walls at the foot of each staircase. Most staircases lead up to three or four sets of chambers. To each set of chambers belong a number of barristers. Each works for himself (or herself, although only about 10 per cent of barristers are women) and together they employ a clerk who negotiates their fees with the solicitors who engage them. (Barristers are only allowed to work for solicitors, and may not be engaged directly by the public.) At the top of each staircase are one or two apartments, usually the home of a judge or a senior barrister.

Middle Temple Hall, opened by Queen Elizabeth I in the 1570s, is on your right as you enter Fountain Court. Shakespeare's *Twelfth Night* was staged here in 1601, under the magnificent oak double hammerbeam roof. The small table in front of the Bench Table on the platform is nicknamed the 'Cupboard' and is thought to be made of wood from Francis Drake's *Golden Hind.*

Inner Temple

Turn right from Fountain Court down Middle Temple Lane and then left along Crown Office Row. On the right are the lovely Inner Temple Gardens, which must surely possess one of the best cared-for lawns in London. A notice proclaims that the gardens are private, but I once ate a sandwich lunch on a bench there without being hauled up in front of a judge. Charles Lamb, author of *Tales from Shakespeare,* was born here. He loved the Temple and spent much of his life here. The fountain in Inner Temple Gardens was put up in his memory, and is inscribed 'Lawyers were children once'.

Temple Church

At the end of Crown Office Row, turn left and immediately right, past the Buttery, once part of the refectory where the Knights ate their meals, to the Temple Church. This was built by the Knights Templar in 1185 but has been much restored since then. The chancel and the nave are known respectively as the 'Oblong' and the 'Round', for reasons that become obvious once you go inside. The circular nave, which imitates the Church of the Holy Sepulchre in Jerusalem, is one of only five in England.

King's Bench Walk

Now continue straight on to the end of Church Court and out into King's Bench Walk. The tall red brick houses (most of which were designed by Wren after their predecessors had been destroyed in the Great Fire), set well back around a wide square, make this one of London's most elegant and spacious spots.

Our way out of Temple is through the gateway into Tudor Street about halfway down the east side of King's Bench Walk (on the left as you face the river). If this is closed you will have to make your way along Fleet Street and rejoin the walk at St Bride's Church.

Northcliffe House

Walk straight down Tudor Street. Northcliffe House on the left is the headquarters of the *Daily Mail* and the *Mail on Sunday* (Lord Northcliffe founded the *Mail* in 1896), at number 23 are the offices of *Punch,* and in Bouverie Street the *Sun* and the *News of the World* are produced.

Whitefriars   The streets round here have a much more distinguished history than their relatively undistinguished appearance would suggest. As is often the case, street names give the game away: in this case Whitefriar Street and Carmelite Street. In the Middle Ages, an order of monks known as the Carmelites – also called Whitefriars, because they wore a white mantle, or coat, over their brown robes – established a priory in Fleet Street. By the time the monasteries were dissolved in the late 1530s, the monks had erected a large number of buildings, and a garden ran right down to the river. The site was parcelled out among the royal household – the king's armourer and his physician were the principal beneficiaries – and no evidence of the priory now remains above ground. Beneath the presses of the *Sun,* however, some 2½ metres (8 feet) below ground level, a lovely 14th-century crypt and the paving of the cloister walk are preserved. They can be visited, but only by prior arrangement with the newspaper.

Bridewell   Immediately east of the former monastery you reach another site of great distinction: Bridewell, which started as a royal palace and finished as a prison. Bridewell was built on the banks of the river Fleet for Henry VIII in 1520. As early as 1553 it was given away, to the City of London, which turned the palace into a prison and a hospital, and so it remained for the next 300 years (it was rebuilt after the Great Fire). It was not perhaps London's grimmest place of punishment, for a prison doctor was provided there long before any other prison had one, and the prisoners even had straw for their beds.

Fleet River   At the end of Tudor Street turn left into New Bridge Street. Number 14 is on the site of the main entrance to Bridewell. The Fleet river, which rises in the northern heights of Hampstead, near Kenwood (see walk 13), still runs here, beneath the pavement. It was enclosed in 1766, having been used as a rubbish dump by all and sundry for several centuries. There is an excellent wholefood restaurant called Food for Health at the end of Blackfriars Lane opposite.

St Bride's Church   A left turn along Bride Lane brings you suddenly up against St Bride's Church, one of London's most splendid churches, at least from the outside. The interior was restored in a rather uninspiring fashion after the church was gutted in an air raid during the Second World War. National newspapers footed much of the bill, for St Bride's is known as the journalists' church. The exterior is one of Wren's masterpieces: in particular the spire, with its four arcades, each smaller than the one below, surmounted by an obelisk and a ball and vane. A local pastrycook, one Mr Rich, was inspired to design a tiered wedding cake modelled on the spire – and found that he had originated a wedding-day tradition.

The real treasures of St Bride's are in the crypt. The bombing revealed the remains of a large Roman house, and these and the foundations of no less than seven different churches built here between the 6th and 17th centuries are on display in the Crypt Museum. There are also exhibits on the early history of printing in the area. Outside, the churchyard is a good picnic spot.

Fleet Street   Turn left along Fleet Street from Bride Lane, past the offices of the *Daily Express* and the *Daily Telegraph*. Printers and booksellers moved to Fleet Street, which had been a main thoroughfare for centuries connecting the City and Westminster, almost as soon as printing began in England. The first was Wynkyn de Worde, a pupil of Caxton, who came here in about 1500 and set up shop at the sign of the Sun near the entrance to Shoe Lane. The first newspapers were produced 200 years later.

Ye Olde Cheshire Cheese   Turn right up Wine Office Court past Ye Olde Cheshire Cheese. Many writers and men of letters ate here during the 18th and 19th centuries including, very probably, Samuel Johnson, who compiled a dictionary of the English language. A parrot with the inevitable name of Polly used to live in the inn; when it died in 1926 at the age of 40, obituaries appeared in no less than 200 newspapers.

Gough Square   At the end of Wine Office Court – so called because an office that issued licences to sell wine was situated here – turn left into Gough Square. This is the nicest of the little squares and passages on this side of Fleet Street, and it has a pleasant atmosphere; modern buildings have spoilt the rest. Dr Johnson lived in a house at the far end of the square between 1748 and 1759; it is now a museum. The independent London Broadcasting Company (LBC), has its studios here, and music and chat waft around the square.

Red Lion Court Turn right at the end of the square, then immediately left and left again down Red Lion Court back into Fleet Street. Above number 18 Red Lion Court you can see an old firemark; an outstretched hand is dousing a fire with a jug of water, with the words *Allere Flammam* around it.

Fleet Street Continue west along Fleet Street. Buildings of interest are El Vino's at number 49, a favourite wine bar among journalists, where the management has long refused to serve women at the bar; Prince Henry's Room at number 17, a lovely oak-panelled room with the three feathers of the Prince of Wales and the letters P.H. in the ceiling; and the half-timbered Inner Temple Gateway. The Romanian Orthodox community worships at St Dunstan's Church on the right-hand side.

Temple Bar In the middle of the road, where Fleet Street becomes the Strand, an ugly monument marks the site of Temple Bar. The Bar was one of the gateways into the City from Westminster. The structure built by Christopher Wren survives – but in very poor condition and not here, where it stood for 200 years, but 50 kilometres (30 miles) or so north of London, where it was re-erected, having been dismantled to make way for the increasing traffic. The heads of traitors, boiled in salt to prevent birds eating them, used to be strung up on spikes on the Bar as a grisly warning.

Temple Bar marks the western boundary of the City. By tradition, when the monarch has a ceremonial engagement in the City, she stops here to ask the Lord Mayor's permission to enter. (It is never refused, but the City likes to maintain its sense of independence!) The Lord Mayor's sword of state is then carried at the front of the royal procession, to show that the monarch is under the Lord Mayor's protection.

On the left-hand side is the Wig and Pen Club in a timber-framed building at number 229 Strand. Its members are lawyers and writers. Lloyds Bank has some magnificent ornate tile decorations. On the right are the Royal Courts of Justice (the Law Courts), opened in 1882 when they moved from Westminster Hall (see walk 2). About 60 courts are available in the main building, and there are various extensions. Civil cases are heard here; for criminal trials you have to go to the Central Criminal Court in the Old Bailey (see walk 8). Twinings Coffee House at number 216 has been in business since 1706, although sadly you can no longer eat or drink there.

St Clement Danes

The church ahead in the centre of the road is well known to all children, and to all adults who have any recollections of their nursery days. It is St Clement Danes, which claims to be the St Clement's Church of the 'Oranges and Lemons' nursery rhyme, and which supports that claim in an annual service when the children of St Clement Danes primary school are each given an orange and a lemon. Apparently an annual toll of oranges and lemons was paid to the church so that cargoes from ships moored in the Thames could be carried through the churchyard to Clare Market just to the north. Many people believe, however, that St Clement Eastcheap in the City is more likely to be the church referred to in the rhyme. Whichever is the case, the bells of this St Clement's do play the rhymes every three hours. The building was gutted during the Second World War, and afterwards it became the official church of the Royal Air Force. The interior has a rather impersonal atmosphere, with many military monuments and memorials.

Now retrace your steps past the Law Courts and turn left up Bell Yard. Cross Carey Street, where bankruptcy hearings are held, and continue up Star Yard to see one of London's quaintest sights – and a useful one too, but only for men. Hard against the wall of Lincoln's Inn is an old-fashioned cast-iron urinal, rather like the ones that used to stand in the streets of Paris. Turn right down Chichester Rents – an odd-sounding name but entirely logical: this street led to the London palace of the Bishops of Chichester, and buildings to rent were constructed along it.

Chancery Lane A little way back down Chancery Lane to the right is the Public Record Office, where legal and government records dating back to the Norman Conquest are stored. The museum here displays interesting documents, including the *Domesday Book* and Shakespeare's will. (Note that this museum will be closed until early 1986.)

London Silver Vaults Turn left from Chichester Rents into Chancery Lane and walk up as far as Southampton Buildings on the right. Here are the London Silver Vaults. You descend a staircase, pass through several sets of strong doors, and find yourself in a long corridor in the shape of a square with shops leading off it. This is where some of London's best-known silver-dealers trade. The shops – they are more like giant safes than normal stores – are filled with teapots and rings, jewellery and statues and anything that can be made of silver. The atmosphere is airless and oppressive: perhaps it is something to do with all those riches – more than you and I could ever dream of – embodied in sometimes rather unattractive objects.

Lincoln's Inn Back in the relatively fresh air of London's streets, retrace your steps down Chancery Lane and turn right into Lincoln's Inn through the gatehouse. If the gate is shut, you will have to walk north up Chancery Lane, turn left along High Holborn, left down Great Turnstile and along the east side of Lincoln's Inn Fields, to enter Lincoln's Inn through the main gates.

Lincoln's Inn is another of the Inns of Court (the fourth, Gray's Inn, is not visited on this walk). It is worth spending a little time looking around; like Temple, Lincoln's Inn is delightfully secluded and quiet. You can picnic on the beautiful lawn just behind the New Hall between 12.00 and 2.30 pm on Mondays to Fridays, when the gardens are open to the public 'for the enjoyment of rest and quiet'. The Old Hall dates from the late 15th century and has a collarbeam roof; the Old Buildings are Tudor and have lovely brickwork; the Chapel was built in 1623, and may well have been designed by Inigo Jones; New Square is a fine late 17th century square; and the New Hall and Library date from the mid-19th century. Take care to maintain a proper demeanour here, though. Notices warn that people 'making a noise within this Inn' will be 'removed'!

Lincoln's Inn Fields

Leave Lincoln's Inn by the main gate and cross into Lincoln's Inn Fields, one of central London's most pleasant and elegant squares. There is a bandstand, a snack bar and even tennis courts, as well as plenty of grass on which to lie down and relax. The square was created in the mid-17th century, after disputed attempts to build over the entire area led to a compromise by which houses were to be constructed round the edges but the fields in the centre left clear.

Sir John Soane's Museum

Although none of the original houses remains, some that were built in the 18th century are still standing. Among them is the house – or rather the three houses – in which the architect Sir John Soane lived between 1792 and 1837, and which is now Sir John Soane's Museum. Numbers 12, 13 and 14 look quite normal from the outside. Go inside, however, and you will find an incredible treasure trove of pictures, furniture, manuscripts, statues, clocks, archaeological remains and relics of all kinds. Sir John was not simply an architect: he was also a collector – an avid collector of almost anything of historical, artistic or archaeological interest that came his way. His home (he lived in number 12 first, then bought 13 and later still number 14) is preserved more or less as it was when he died. As soon as you enter you sense the force of his personality. Here is a collection that reflects the taste of a single man, not of a group.

It is not merely the objects it contains that make the museum so unusual. The very layout of the building is complex, almost disturbing. You continually bump into dead ends, or come across startling views and changes of perspective. The Monk's Parlour is a Gothick fantasy with a window through which you can see the tomb of an imaginary monastic priest. Another fascinating room is the Picture Room. Not only are all four walls lined with pictures; three of them consist of hinged plates that open up to reveal another wall of pictures behind. The south wall has two such planes, with a view over a recess behind. Among the celebrated pictures in the room are Hogarth's eight paintings called *The Rake's Progress*. One shows the Rake incarcerated in Bridewell Prison, the site of which we passed earlier in the walk. Sir John Soane's Museum is one of the London museums which you should not miss.

The Old Curiosity Shop Now walk across or around Lincoln's Inn Fields (there is a useful tea bar on the west side) and down Portsmouth Street in the south-west corner. The Old Curiosity Shop on the left-hand side is over 400 years old and was featured in Dickens's novel of the same name. It sells souvenirs of London. A right turn along Sheepfold Street and then another turn right into Portugal Street brings you out into Kingsway, where the walk ends. Holborn Underground Station is a little way up Kingsway on the right.

Middle Temple Hall

Tel: 01-353 4355
Opening times: Mondays to Fridays 10.00-11.30am, 3.00-4.00pm; closed Bank Holidays

Temple Church

Opening times: Mondays to Fridays 10.00am-4.00pm; closed Bank Holidays

St Bride's Church and Crypt Museum

Fleet Street
London EC4Y 8AV
Tel: 01-353 1301
Opening times: Mondays to Saturdays 9.00am-5.00pm; Sundays 9.00am-7.30pm

London Silver Vaults

Chancery House
Chancery Lane
London WC2
Tel: 01-242 3844
Opening times: Mondays to Fridays 9.00am-5.30pm; Saturdays 9.00am-12.30pm; closed Bank Holidays

53

Lincoln's Inn Chapel

Opening times: Mondays to Fridays 12.30-2.30pm;
closed Bank Holidays
To see other parts of the Inn, apply in writing to the
Treasury Office

Sir John Soane's Museum

13 Lincoln's Inn Fields
London WC2A 3BP
Tel: 01-405 2107
Opening times: Tuesdays to Saturdays 10.00am-5.00pm

6   SOUTHWARK

Start: St Katharine's Dock
Underground: Tower Hill
Buses: 23, 42, 56, 78

Finish: Blackfriars Bridge
Underground: Blackfriars
Buses: 45, 63, 76, 109, 141, 184

Distance: 4 kilometres (2½ miles)

Places to sit down: Churchyard, Southwark Cathedral
    In front of Bankside Power Station

Eating places: *SS Great Yarmouth, St Katherine's Dock*
    Vegetarian Dining Room, Cathedral Street

Lavatories: Corner of Joiner Street and Tooley Street
    By passageway under Blackfriars Railway
    Bridge

This is a walk through the heart of one of London's fastest changing areas, the city's original dockland. For centuries vessels bound for London would make their way up the Thames to the Pool of London, that stretch of river immediately below London Bridge. Smaller craft would tie up alongside the quays, while larger vessels would moor amidstream and discharge their cargoes into barges, known on the Thames as lighters.

The river scene in the late 18th century was becoming increasingly busy. Almost all the capital's coal, minerals, textiles and food, and its luxuries such as silks, ivory and spices, came by sea. 13,949 vessels moored in the Pool in 1794. Just 30 years later the number had increased to 23,618. So great was the traffic that space was literally running out; the quays and warehouses were full, the river a forest of masts.

To cope with the overcrowding, and also to prevent the pilfering which abstracted up to a third of the goods brought in by boat, a series of enclosed docks was constructed further downstream, between the Tower of London and Greenwich. The first were the West India Docks, opened in 1802 (see also walk 11), and another of the docks was St Katharine's Dock, which is where this walk begins.

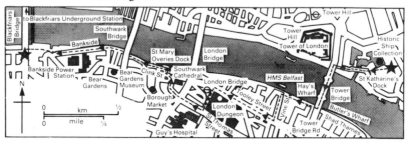

St Katharine's Dock

The Dock lies just east of Tower Bridge. If you are coming from Tower Hill Underground Station, walk straight down to the riverbank past the entrance to the Tower, and then turn left along the river and pass under Tower Bridge. Beyond the pétanque ground – thoughtfully placed here by the site's developers (but who in London plays French *boules?*) – you will reach the lock that opens to admit vessels to the dock.

St Katharine's was opened in 1828. There were two large docks, the Western and the Eastern, divided by an entrance basin and the Ivory Warehouse, which was added in the 1850s. Warehouses six storeys tall and supported on iron columns lined the long quayside, so close that the cranes on each floor could reach straight into the holds of vessels moored alongside. The vaults underneath the docks provided 42 kilometres (26 miles) of storage space. Every article imaginable was stored there: spices, ivory, tea, tobacco, wine, carpets, sugar, silk, opium, marble, scent. In 1900 the dock handled 9 million tonnes of shipping, and the vaults held 15,000 pipes of wines and 10,000 puncheons of rum.

St Katharine's Dock was closed in 1968 and has now been redeveloped to include the World Trade Centre, a large hotel and a yacht marina. Sadly not all the warehouses have survived. The Ivory House, in whose vaults prisoners were held before being transported to Australia, has been turned into shops and luxury flats, and another has become the Dickens Inn. The whole area is something of a disappointment – rather twee and without much historical atmosphere.

Historic Ship Collection
To make up for that, however, the Historic Ship Collection, which occupies part of the old Eastern Dock, is fascinating. The best-known vessel here is *RRS Discovery* (RRS stands for Royal Research Ship), which was the floating headquarters of Scott's first Antarctic expedition (not the one from which he failed to return). The ship is being restored as it was in 1925, and on board there is a great deal of interest to see. The ship was immensely strong, as she had to be to take the strain of being trapped in the polar ice for many months at a time: you can see the vertical oak frame between the inner and outer pine planking.

Although the other vessels in the collection are not quite as celebrated as *Discovery*, most are typical of the thousands of vessels that worked around the British coast until a few decades ago. Especially interesting is the Great Yarmouth herring drifter *Lydia Eve*, with her huge fish hold into which the freshly caught herring were tipped. There is also the steam coaster *Robin*, the last survivor of her kind, brought back to England after working under the Spanish flag for 74 years. Thousands of coasters like *Robin* carried cargoes of all kinds between British and Irish ports, and to and from ocean-going vessels, also occasionally making cross-Channel trips.

Just outside the collection, by the Dickens Inn, there is a pleasant ice-cream and coffee place on board the *SS Yarmouth*. There is also a café (though not an especially good one) just beyond the pétanque ground, on the far side of Tower Bridge.

Tower Bridge The walk continues across Tower Bridge, which was completed as recently as 1894 to handle some of the enormous volume of traffic using London Bridge. The central spans open to let vessels pass through – nowadays only about three or four times a week on average. By contrast in the first month in 1894, the bridge opened no less than 655 times. Queues of traffic built up whenever the bridge closed, even though each opening only took between three and five minutes. One remarkable day in 1952, something went badly wrong with the warning signals, and a bus driver found himself on the bridge as it started to open. With great presence of mind he accelerated over the widening gap and slithered to safety down the opposite span.

Although originally the bridge was raised and lowered by hydraulic machinery, nowadays it is operated by electricity; its story is told in an exhibition inside the North and South Towers. You ascend the North Tower in a lift, and look at displays explaining the structural and hydraulic engineering of the bridge. Then you cross the Thames on enclosed walkways with magnificent views up and downstream. It's well worth crossing both walkways. The South Tower houses exhibitions on Thames bridges and on the construction of Tower Bridge itself. The final stage in the visit is to the original machinery used to raise and lower the bridge: boilers, steam and hydraulic engines and accumulators all beautifully preserved in full working order.

Whether or not you visit the Tower Bridge exhibition, cross to the south bank and take the steps that lead from the bridge down to the riverbank. As the docks expanded in the early 19th century, large warehouses were built all along the riverfront to store raw materials and manufac-tured goods shipped in from overseas. In the 1950s and 1960s most activity in the Port of London moved downstream to the Tilbury area, where the river is deep enough to accommodate modern vessels and there was land available to build up-to-date container terminals. Like the enclosed docks, the warehouses fell derelict, and for a decade or more the streets here lay crumbling and neglected, although flats and studios were built in some of the warehouses.

Shad Thames Now, in the mid-1980s, all that has changed, and here some of London's most prestigious current building projects are under way. Immediately to the east of Tower Bridge, along Shad Thames, Butler's Wharf, where the Courage Brewery used to stand, is being turned into an area of private housing. The old brewery chimney is being preserved, or at least that part of it which is visible above roof level. As often happens in this part of London, north or south of the river, building work revealed a Roman site, in this case a large civic structure with at least ten rooms; elsewhere on the site a Roman necklace was found, 61 centimetres (24 inches) long and made of 35 blue faience beads.

Hay's Wharf Hay's Wharf, that stretch of riverbank between Tower Bridge and London Bridge, is the oldest wharf in the Pool of London. Cold storage was developed here in the 1860s. The redevelopment project along the wharf is known as London Bridge City; building is progressing from west to east. The first part is expected to be completed by the end of 1986, by which time a public park on the river's edge near Tower Bridge will also be ready. Among much new building – including two office-blocks built in flame-textured granite and glass – the original façade of the Hay's Dock building erected in 1857 will be preserved, under the new title of Hay's Galleria.

HMS Belfast Our walk takes the riverbank path west from Tower Bridge towards *HMS Belfast. Belfast,* the largest and one of the most powerful cruisers ever built for the Royal Navy, took part in December 1943 in one of the most celebrated

engagements of the Second World War, the Battle of the
North Cape, in which the German *Scharnhorst* was sunk;
she was also present off Normandy on D-Day in June
1944. After the war she spent a lot of time in the Far East.
When her active career ended in 1963 she was destined for
the scrapyard, and was only saved through the efforts of
the Imperial War Museum.

The tour of the ship takes up to two hours. You can see
her armaments, and the sophisticated Fire Control Table
which was used to make the calculations that enabled the
gunners to hit a moving target from a moving vessel up to
23 kilometres (14 miles) away. The messdecks, galley,
bridges, punishment cells and operations room are all on
display, and below are the massive, gleaming boilers and
engines.

For naval and military enthusiasts, adults or children,
and those interested in the Second World War, a visit to
HMS Belfast is a must. Others may prefer to admire the
vessel and her magnificent backdrop of the Tower, the
Monument and St Paul's, from the riverbank.

**Tower
Subway**
From *HMS Belfast* walk down Vine Street and turn right
into Tooley Street. The square brick building about
halfway down Vine Street on the right-hand side is the
southern exit of the Tower Subway, which runs for 408
metres (1,340 feet) under the Thames from Tower Hill.
Opened in 1869, it was originally used by cable-hauled
trams, but was soon converted to a pedestrian tunnel. After
Tower Bridge opened the tunnel was closed and is now
used for water mains.

The walk west along Tooley Street is accompanied not just
by the roar of traffic but also by the rumbling of trains in
and out of London Bridge Station. The original line here
was the first railway built in London, running along a 6-
kilometre (3¾-mile) viaduct through Deptford to Greenwich. London Bridge was thus the capital's first terminus,
although it beat Euston by only a few months, and Euston,
when it did open, was a far grander place.

On the right, now submerged beneath the London
Bridge City development, are two streets known as English
and Irish Ground. Navvies building the London &

Greenwich Railway were lodged here in two separate camps according to nationality.

The London Dungeon
In the arches underneath the railway you come to one of London's most popular tourist attractions: the London Dungeon. The Dungeon is a museum of every conceivable – and inconceivable – horror. The depictions are carefully re-searched and dramatically staged, and although they do not come up to date (where are the gas chambers and the atom bomb?) they do show just how cruel humankind can be. The Dungeon is not for the squeamish, nor should one take young children there; but clearly many people do enjoy it.

The Old Operating Theatre
For something far more genuinely horrific, turn left into Joiner Street and then right into St Thomas Street. On the left is Guy's Hospital, and on the right is a short row of elegant houses. These are all that remains of old St Thomas's Hospital, which occupied this site for over 600 years until it moved to Lambeth when it had to make way for an extension of the railway from London Bridge to Charing Cross.

And thereby hangs a tale. The loft of St Thomas's Church had been used as a herb garret, in which medicinal herbs were stored and dried. In 1821 a new operating theatre for female patients was created out of part of the herb garret. When the hospital moved, the way upstairs was blocked off, and the operating theatre was forgotten for almost a century.

Now, however, the theatre has been restored to its original condition – and how gruesome that was! Small wonder is it that many people in the early 19th century preferred death to the surgeon's knife. The surgeon worked in an apron stained with blood from previous patients, and washing facilities were practically non-existent; spectators watched from the steeply raked benches around the operating table, underneath which a sawdust-filled box caught the blood flowing from the patient. When it was full the surgeon called for 'more sawdust'. In the herb garret there is an interesting exhibition on the history of Guy's and St Thomas's Hospitals and on the develop-ment of medicine and surgery. This is one of London's least known and most interesting small museums.

Southwark Cathedral Walk to the end of St Thomas Street, cross the road and make your way into Southwark Cathedral churchyard, which is a pleasant place for a picnic. The faint smell of fruit and vegetables comes from Borough Market which, like all wholesale markets, operates in the early morning.

The cathedral dates from the 13th century, although it has been much altered since then, and replaced an earlier building, St Mary Overie (St Mary Overies Dock, see below, is close by) that was erected in 1106. The interior is pleasant and simple, with many monuments. John Harvard, who was baptised here in 1608 and went on to found Harvard University in the USA, is commemorated in the Harvard Chapel. Look for the funny faces on the bosses and also for the memorial to Lockyer, a pill-merchant, who died in 1672:

His VIRTUES and his PILLS are so well known
That envy can't confine them under stone.

Southwark This is the heart of Southwark, London's oldest suburb, which has existed since Roman times. (For London Bridge, see walk 11.) Southwark has been famous for many things: for its prisons (there were no less than seven); for its breweries and inns (Chaucer's Canterbury Pilgrims set out from here, and it was a natural port of call for travellers making for London from the south); for its 'stews' (as brothels were then called); for its churches and churchmen (many bishops had their London houses here); for its bear-baiting; and for its theatre. Many of these flourished because Southwark was outside the direct control of the City.

St Mary Overies Dock Just beyond the cathedral is another huge rebuilding project at St Mary Overies Dock, which is going up on the site of the 13th-century London palace of the Bishops of Winchester. This in turn was built on a Roman site that included a large public bath and perhaps also a club for off-duty Roman legionaries. A magnificent Roman fresco was found here during the excavations for the modern building, which will incorporate the massive west wall of the great hall of the Bishops' Palace with its lovely rose windows.

There is a pleasant and not over-expensive Vegetarian

Dining Room (open lunchtimes and evening, Tuesdays to Fridays) at number 1 Cathedral Street. Newspapers and magazines are supplied for diners to read.

Clink The walk continues down Winchester Street, right into Stoney Street and then left into Clink Street, where some of the 19th-century warehouses still stand. The Bishops of Winchester originally owned the Clink Prison, which fell into disuse in the mid-17th century and was burnt down in 1780. It was, apparently, by no means the nastiest of Southwark's prisons, and has achieved fame mainly through its name, now used as the slang term for any prison.

Bear Gardens Museum The path follows the river upstream, past the Bankside pub and under Southwark Bridge. The streets around here are run down, but the views across the river to St Paul's are splendid. In the early 17th century this was London's playground: here there were bear gardens – where not only bears but cocks, dogs and bulls were set upon each other – and theatres (many well-known actors lived here). To the left just past the bridge you come to a street called Bear Gardens, down which, on the left-hand side, you reach the Bear Gardens Museum of the Shakespearean Stage and Arts Centre.

The museum provides an interesting but rather academic account of the early English theatre up to the mid-17th century, with a lot of information about the Globe Theatre, where many of Shakespeare's plays were first seen. Performances took place in the afternoons, since there was no lighting, and most of the audience sat or stood in the open air, although the stage itself was covered. Scenery was virtually non-existent. Above the museum is a replica of a small early 17th-century theatre where performances are often given.

In Shakespeare's day, the theatre was a genuinely popular art, and all types of people came to performances: Southwark locals as well as rich merchants and towns-people from across the river. A little further west along Bankside you pass the spot where the American actor Sam Wanamaker is hoping to build a full-size reconstruction of the Globe.

Bankside The final stretch of the walk runs west along the river past the derelict building of the memorably named Jones-Willcox Wire-Bound Hose Company Limited and Cardinal's Wharf. Christopher Wren is said to have lived in one of the houses here while St Paul's was being built, and Catherine of Aragon, the first of Henry VIII's six wives, took shelter here when she first arrived in England. There are stone seats among the gardens in front of Bankside Power Station – opened as recently as 1963 but already out of use – and from here there are splendid views across to St Paul's and the City Heliport which is in fact a large barge in the river.

Blackfriars Bridge The walk continues under Blackfriars Railway Bridge – there used to be two railway bridges next to each other, but the western one has been demolished – and out on to the road bridge, where the walk ends. The pub opposite, Doggetts, commemorates Doggetts Coat and Badge Race, the annual rowing race which covers a course of 7 kilometres (4½ miles) along the Thames. The contest is the oldest annual event in British sport and was originated by Thomas Doggett, a comic actor and manager of the Drury Lane Theatre, who left money for the prizes when he died in 1721.

Historic Ship Collection (Maritime Trust)
52 St Katharine's Way
London E1 9LB
Tel: 01-481 0043
Opening times: April to October: daily 10.00 am-6.00 pm; October to April: daily 10.00 am-5.00 pm

Tower Bridge
London SE1 2UP
Tel: 01-403 5386; 01-403 3761; 01-407 0922
Opening times: April to October: daily 10.00 am-6.30 pm; November to March: daily 10.00 am-4.45 pm; last admission 45 minutes before closing time

HMS Belfast
Symons Wharf
Vine Lane
Tooley Street
London SE1 2JH
Tel: 01-407 6434
Opening times: 20 March to 31 October: daily
11.00 am-5.50 pm; 1 November to 19 March: daily
11.00 am-4.30 pm; last admission 30 minutes before
closing time; closed some Bank Holidays

The London Dungeon
28/34 Tooley Street
London SE1 2SZ
Tel: 01-403 0606
Opening times: April to September: daily
10.00 am-5.30 pm; October to March: daily
10.00 am-4.30 pm

Old Operating Theatre and Herb Garret
Guy's Hospital
St Thomas Street
London SE1 9RT
Tel: 01-407 7600 extension 2739 or 3149
Opening times: Mondays, Wednesdays and Fridays
only 12.30-4.00 pm; at other times by appointment

Bear Gardens Museum of the Shakespearean Stage
1 Bear Gardens
Bankside
London SE1 9EB
Tel: 01-928 6342
Opening times: Tuesdays to Saturdays
10.00 am-5.30 pm; Sundays 2.00-6.00 pm

7　AROUND BANK

Start: The Monument
Underground: Monument
Buses: 8A, 10, 35, 40, 40A, 44, 47, 48

Finish: Mansion House Underground Station
Buses: 6, 9, 11, 15, 18, 23, 76, 95, 149, 184, 513

Distance: 4 kilometres (2½ miles)

Places to sit down: Churchyard, St Mary-at-Hill
Churchyard, St Peter upon
Cornhill Courtyard underneath
Woolgate House, Moorgate

Eating places: Leadenhall Market
Cheapside

Lavatories: Guildhall Yard

This walk winds through the heart of the City of London, passing some of its most famous landmarks. The City today is an extraordinary place: one of the world's most important financial centres (some would say *the* most important), yet with hardly more than a few thousand residents. It is lively and urgent during weekdays – you can almost feel the money being made – but eerily deserted after office hours and at weekends. Although the off-duty City does have its charm, this walk and the next – *Around St Paul's* – are best done on weekdays.

For a long time the City *was* London. The Romans built their first bridge here, more or less where London Bridge stands now, and constructed their city on and around two hills, Cornhill and St Paul's. London Bridge itself was the only river crossing until the 18th century. In the Middle Ages, if you were a Londoner you lived and worked and died within the square mile of the City. Until about 1850, when its population was still over 100,000, the City was a mixed community, many businessmen and craftsmen living above or very near their workplaces. People only began to move out to the suburbs in large numbers in the second half of the 19th century.

Two calamities have marked the landscape of the City: the Great Fire of 1666 and the Blitz of 1940 and 1941. The Fire burnt for five days; it devastated well over 160 hectares (400 acres), including 87 churches and 13,200 houses, but only claimed nine lives. (There is an excellent recreation of the Fire in the Museum of London.) Reconstruction took place literally from scratch, although the medieval street pattern was retained. From about 1840 the late 17th-century city was rebuilt bit by bit, with increasingly imposing warehouses, shops and office blocks. Some new thoroughfares were made, but on the whole the streets still ran much as they did in medieval times. The eight-month London Blitz did at least as much damage as the Great Fire. Unfortunately post-war rebuilding, which is still going on, has not been particularly sympathetic, and towering temples of glass have obliterated many old squares and courts. This walk takes in some of the small corners that do remain.

Before we start, a word about two important City institutions which are much in evidence on the walk. The Court of Common Council, the main local council that runs the City, is made up of 133 Councilmen representing 25 tiny areas called wards. As you would expect in an area of 274 hectares (677 acres), many of the wards are tiny, and cover just a few streets. As you explore, look out for small oval plaques set into walls; these name the local ward.

The oldest of the City Livery Companies date back 800 years. Livery Companies were guilds formed by groups of craftsmen or traders who got together to control work in their profession; they determined prices and wages; checked that their members were producing good-quality work; looked after the elderly and sick; built a Hall as their headquarters; and, most important of all, controlled entry into the profession. Not only are many Livery Companies still in existence – there are currently 94, of which 17 have been formed in the last 50 years – they still play an important part in their trade.

Monument And now to the walk itself. Start at the 62-metre (202-foot) high Monument, on Fish Street Hill, designed by Christopher Wren. It is, as you might expect, a monument to the Great Fire and is said to be exactly 202 feet from the spot in Pudding Lane where the fire is believed to have started. The 311-step climb is well worth the effort; the views from the top are spectacular, and you will see how construction in the last 20 years or so has completely changed the City skyline. Imagine the scene 300 years ago when, except for St Paul's Cathedral, this was London's tallest building.

Billingsgate Now walk east along Monument Street, cross Pudding
Market Lane – careful with those matches! – and turn left into cobbled Lovat Lane. The derelict building surmounted by the figure of Britannia on the far side of Lower Thames Street at the end of Monument Street is Billingsgate fish market, which moved from here to a site on the Isle of Dogs in 1982. The area round here is all a bit fishy. The building at the corner of Lovat Lane has a weather vane on top representing a bawley, a boat which was used until 1950 to catch whitebait in the Thames, and at the church of St Mary-at-Hill, halfway up Lovat Lane, the Billingsgate fish merchants hold their annual harvest festival service.

Turn right from Lovat Lane along the passage by the church and then left into St Mary-at-Hill. The secluded churchyard on the left has some seats, and is a good picnic spot. Cross Eastcheap and continue straight on, then turn right into Fenchurch Street and left into Cullum Street, past some rather uninteresting office blocks. Another turn right brings you into Lime Street.

Lime Street is so called because there were once limekilns here. City street names are full of interesting historical associations. Some are simple enough; as you would expect, there was a clutch of bakers' shops along Bread Street. Others are less obvious nowadays. Cannon

69

Street has nothing to do with armaments, but is a corruption of Candlewick Street, which in turn comes from Candelewrithstrete, the street of candle-makers.

Lloyd's   Ahead on the right is the extension building of Lloyd's (not open to the public). This is one of the City's most famous financial institutions. It started in the late 17th century as a coffee house at which merchants, sea captains and shipowners gathered. From that a maritime insurance business developed, and today members of Lloyd's – who are known as underwriters – accept every kind of insurance risk. The underwriters trade in the Underwriting Room, where a ship's bell, known as the Lutine Bell, is rung when an important announcement is to be made; two strokes signify good news, one bad.

Leadenhall Market   Turn left shortly before Lloyd's into Leadenhall Market, which, although it specializes in meat and poultry as it always has done, has a good number of general shops and some cafés. The lovely market building, all glass and cast iron, dates from 1881, but the market itself goes back to the 14th century.

St Peter upon Cornhill   From Leadenhall Market turn right into Gracechurch Street (the magnificent interior of Barclays Bank at number 9 is worth a quick look) and then left into St Peter's Alley. You could picnic in the churchyard of St Peter upon Cornhill, one of the churches Wren built in the City after the Great Fire.

Roman London   Follow the passage round and turn left into Cornhill. Since Fenchurch Street we have been walking through – or perhaps one should say above – the central focus of Londinium, Roman London. Here stood the huge basilica (only Rome's was larger) which housed the courts and administrative offices, and the forum, where citizens came for meetings and to do their shopping.

Change Alley   From Cornhill, the route runs through a series of tiny alleyways that, even though they are hemmed in by modern buildings, still follow the route of the original medieval street. Turn left into Ball Court, past Simpsons, the well-known City eating-place, and then right into Castle Court. Then it is left into Birchin Lane, second right into Change Alley and straight on as far as you can go; finally a left turn brings you out into Lombard Street. Many of the City's coffee houses were situated in Change Alley, and goods were bought and sold here, fortunes made and lost.

Mansion House A right turn down Lombard Street brings you to a traffic-laden junction that is the focal point of the City. In front of you, slightly to the left, is the Mansion House, the official residence of the Lord Mayor of London. Each year, on the second Saturday in November, the new Lord Mayor processes from here to the Law Courts in the Strand, where he takes his oath of office; the accompanying celebrations, known as the Lord Mayor's Show, are one of the city's most colourful festivities.

Royal Exchange Behind you is the Royal Exchange. The Exchange (it only became Royal in 1844, when Queen Victoria opened the present building) was originally constructed to provide an indoor meeting place for merchants and traders who had previously done business in the open air and in coffee houses in and around Lombard Street. From the 18th century much of it was occupied by the Royal Exchange Assurance Company, which is still there today, although it has acquired the word 'Guardian' at the start of its name. The Exchange's most recent arrival is the London International Financial Futures Exchange. There is a visitors' gallery from which you can watch the members trading fast and furiously on the floor of the Exchange.

Bank of England On the other side of Threadneedle Street is the fortress-like façade of the Bank of England. The Bank has several functions. It is the Government's bank, and the bank of all the other banks such as Barclays and Lloyds. The nations reserves are stored deep in its vaults – many billions of dollars' worth, mostly in foreign currencies but with some gold as well. In England and Wales, only the Bank of England may issue paper currency (in Scotland three separate banks have that right). There is a small museum, but appointments to see it must be made in advance.

Stock Exchange

Now walk along Threadneedle Street (since the 18th century the Bank of England's nickname has been 'The Old Lady of Threadneedle Street') and then bear left into Old Broad Street. On the left is the entrance to the public gallery of the Stock Exchange. There are regular explanatory talks and a film show, and from the gallery you can look down on the brokers and jobbers as they go about their business of buying and selling shares. Most of the time the scene is quite dignified, but sometimes, when a popular share comes on the market, there is a tremendous hubbub. Shares in no less than 2,737 different companies are dealt in here, and on average some 29,000 different transactions are completed here every day, worth together about over £1.5 billion.

National Westminster Tower

A little further up Old Broad Street, turn right into Adams Court, walk under a lovely cast-iron archway and then straight across a pleasant small square. This brings you out at the foot of the National Westminster Tower. Here some statistics are in order. The Tower is Britain's tallest office building – some 2,500 people work here – and Europe's second tallest occupied building. It is 180 metres (600 feet) high, weighs 130,000 tonnes, has nearly 130,000 square feet (12,000 square metres) of windows (all automatically washed), and cost £98 million to build. Inside there are 21 lifts, two of them double-decker, which travel at speeds of between 150 and 430 metres (500 and 1,400 feet) a minute, plus a Document Transporter System along whose 1-kilometre (⅔-mile) track 100 cars deliver mail and documents to 42 outlets throughout the building. From the top there are views over eight counties (though sadly you won't be able to enjoy them, as the public is not admitted); the Tower itself, of course, can be seen from all over London and beyond.

Now turn left from Old Broad Street into Winchester Street, left again down Austin Friars Passage by the side of the United Overseas Bank, and right along Austin Friars. As the street names suggest, the land here once belonged to an Augustinian monastery; after the dissolution of the monasteries, the church (twice rebuilt since then) was passed to the Dutch community.

At the far end of Austin Friars, turn left into Throgmorton Avenue, past Drapers' Gardens (where the Queen and Prince Charles have both planted mulberry bushes) and Drapers' Hall (not open to the public) and then right into Throgmorton Street, by the members' entrance to The Stock Exchange. With luck you may see some traditional City gents, complete with brollies and bowler hats.

Turn right into Angel Court, walk under the buildings at the far end, turn left along Telegraph Street (the Central Telegraph Station was here for 60 years), left again along a passage leading into Tokenhouse Yard and right into King's Arms Yard.

Clock Museum Turn to the right up Moorgate and then left underneath Woolgate House, where a modern City courtyard has been created, with seats, fountains and palms. Then it is right into Basinghall Street, left up the wide steps and left again along Aldermanbury in front of the new Guildhall Library. Just inside on the left is a small Clock Museum with some magnificent timepieces. Look out especially for a silver skull watch said to have belonged to Mary Queen of Scots, the wrist watch Sir Edmund Hillary wore when he climbed Mount Everest in 1953 and a fascinating rolling ball clock made in about 1900. The ball, which replaces the pendulum, runs along grooves in a tilting platform and covers more than 4,000 kilometres (2,500 miles) each year.

Guildhall Round the corner at the end of Aldermanbury you come into Guildhall Yard, a fine open space in front of the Guildhall. The City is governed from the Guildhall, as it has been for over a thousand years, and the annual Lord Mayor's Banquet, given in honour of the 'late' (that is, outgoing) Lord Mayor, is held here on the Monday after the Lord Mayor's Show.

Turn left into Gresham Street and then right into Ironmonger Lane. Underneath number 11, but not open to the public, is a stretch of Roman mosaic pavement. Now go left into St Olave's Court and right into Old Jewry, where a community of Jews lived in the 12th century. Glance down Frederick's Place on the right, where some elegant 18th-century houses have survived. Two hundred years ago many City Streets must have looked like this.

St Mary-le-Bow

At the end of Old Jewry, turn right into Cheapside and walk along to St Mary-le-Bow. Cheapside was the medieval Londoner's main shopping centre, and all the guilds were based in nearby streets. You bought your milk in Dairy Street, your fish in Friday Street (Friday was a meatless day) and had your shoes mended in Cordwainer Street.

St Mary-le-Bow is best known for its bells – those bells within the sound of which, it is said, all true Cockneys are born. It was St Mary's bells that supposedly told Dick Whittington to 'turn again', and for several hundred years they were rung daily to sound the 'retreat from work'. Nowadays the word 'Cockney' is an affectionate term for all Londoners; a few hundred years ago it was not so polite (originally it meant a simpleton or a weakling).

Temple of Mithras

Walk down Bow Lane (formerly known as Hosier Lane and before that as Cordwainer Street after the craftsmen who lived there), then turn left into Watling Street, thought to have been a medieval branch of the original Roman road. At the crossroads go straight ahead into Queen Victoria Street, where the Roman Temple of Mithras, the final stopping-point on this walk, is on the right-hand side, in front of Temple Court.

The Temple is rather a disappointment, although the original ground plan is clear enough. Experts claim that it could have been preserved in its entirety where it was found in 1954, 5.4 metres (18 feet) under the present street level, which might have helped convey more of the original atmosphere. Instead it was reconstructed here, and the finds, which included a marble head of Mithras, a Persian sun-god, and busts of several other deities, were removed to the Museum of London. The Temple was used by Roman soldiers in the 2nd century A.D.

The walk finishes at Mansion House Underground Station, from which walk number 8 starts, a few hundred metres west down Queen Victoria Street.

The Monument

Monument Street
London EC3R 8AH
Tel: 01-626 2717
Opening times: 1 April to 30 September: Mondays to
Fridays 9.00 am-6.00 pm, Saturdays and Sundays
2.00-6.00 pm; 1 October to 31 March: Mondays to
Saturdays 9.00 am-2.00 pm and 3.00-4.00 pm, closed
Sundays; last admission 20 minutes before closing time

Mansion House

Guided tours are normally provided on Tuesdays,
Wednesdays and Thursdays at 11.00 am or 2.00 pm.
Advance booking is required and children under 12
are not admitted. Write to:
The Principal Assistant's Office
The Mansion House
London EC4

London International Financial Futures Exchange

Royal Exchange
London EC3V 3PJ
Tel: 01-623 0444
Opening times: The visitors' gallery is open Mondays to
Fridays 11.45 am-2.00 pm; closed on Bank Holidays

Bank of England

Visits to the Museum by prior arrangement only.
There is a long waiting list, so book well in advance,
by writing to:
Information Division
Bank of England
Threadneedle Street
London EC2R 8AH

Stock Exchange

London EC2N 1HP
(entrance to visitors' gallery in Old Broad Street)
Tel: 01-588 2355
Opening times: The visitors' gallery is open Mondays to Fridays 9.45am-3.15pm; closed on Bank Holidays.
Talks and film shows are held daily at 10.00am, 10.30am, 11.30am, 12.30pm, 1.30pm and 2.30pm.
Advance booking is advisable, although visits can be made without prior appointment. Contact:
Public Relations Department,
Stock Exchange

Guildhall

Guildhall Yard
London EC2P 2EJ
Tel: 01-606 3030
Opening times: Mondays to Saturdays 10.00am-5.00pm; Sundays (May to September) 10.00am-5.00pm; closed on Bank Holidays.
The Library is open Mondays to Saturdays 9.30am-5.00pm
The Clock Museum is open Mondays to Fridays 9.30am-5.00pm

8   AROUND ST PAUL'S

Start: Mansion House Underground Station
Buses: 6, 9, 11, 15, 18, 23, 76, 95, 149, 184, 513

Finish: St Paul's Precincts
Underground: St Paul's
Buses: 4, 8, 22, 25, 141, 501, 502

Distance: 2·8 kilometres (1¾ miles)

Places to sit down: Friar Square and Church Entry,
off Ireland Yard
Charterhouse Square, Postman's Park

Eating places: AA Café, Carter Lane
Food for Health, Blackfriars Lane
Oodles, St Paul's Precincts
Slenders, St Paul's Precincts
Museum of London café

Lavatories: West Smithfield, opposite entrance
to St Bartholomew's Hospital
Paternoster Square, St Paul's Precincts

St Paul's Cathedral is so massive and majestic a presence in the City that you can easily overlook the varied jumble of streets and squares immediately round about. This walk explores some of them, and would go well with a visit to the great cathedral, built by Christopher Wren between 1669 and 1710 after the Great Fire, and the fifth cathedral to be built on this site.

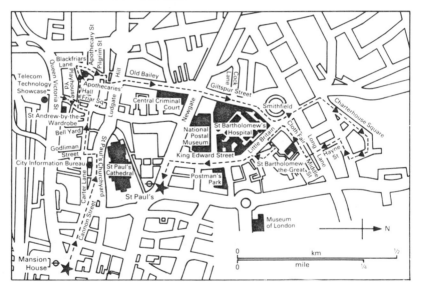

Financial Times Building	From Mansion House station, walk west along Cannon Street towards St Paul's. Number 10, on the left, just after Friday Street, is the *Financial Times* building. The *FT*, which is printed on pink paper, is a leading world newspaper for financial and business news and sells about 225,000 copies every day. There is a splendid astronomical clock above the entrance of the building, indicating not just the minutes and hours, but also the month, the day's date, the current zodiac sign and the phase of the moon. A visual display in one of the windows

shows the current state of the FT Index. This records how the shares of major industrial companies are performing, and is a good indicator of the strength of the country's economy.

St Paul's Choir School Continue along Cannon Street, which now changes its name to St Paul's Churchyard. Before the Great Fire this was the main centre of London's book trade, and many of Shakespeare's plays were first printed here. Through St Augustine's Tower on the right (all that remains of the church of the same name that was bombed in the Second World War) is the entrance to one of London's smallest schools. The boys of St Paul's Choir School (all 38 of them, aged from 8 to 13½) are not only faced with the usual amount of school work; they also sing in most of the cathedral services, rehearse for them, and each pupil learns at least one musical instrument. Their school holidays are rather unusual too: the boys have to stay on at school until after the Christmas Day and the Easter Sunday services are over.

Carter Lane Past the City Information Centre, turn left into Godliman Street and then right into Carter Lane, which is the central spine of a dense warren of tiny streets built after the Great Fire. Amid the 19th-century houses are some lovely older buildings. Bell Yard is on the left, named after the Bell Inn which stood near here and where the only surviving letter to Shakespeare was written (by one Richard Quyney). The AA Café on the right sells cheap food, and the Youth Hostel also on the right was once occupied by the Choir School. Wardrobe Place on the left, now a lovely shaded court, was the site of the Great Wardrobe, a warehouse where the monarchs kept their armour, robes, furniture and so on. Like so much else in the City, it was gutted in the Great Fire.

St Andrew- by-the- Wardrobe Now turn left from Carter Lane down St Andrew's Hill towards the church of St Andrew-by-the-Wardrobe. The church was destroyed in 1666, rebuilt by Wren at a cost of £7,000 16s 11d, destroyed again in 1940 and rebuilt once more 20 years later, by an architect who used Wren's original plans.

Telecom Technology Showcase

From these cramped streets with their feel of history, there is now the chance for an up-to-date diversion at the Telecom Technology Showcase in Queen Victoria Street, across the road from the foot of St Andrew's Hill. The Showcase is a fascinating exhibition of all the latest telecommunications equipment. The contrast with the early days of the telephone, when the operator had to put through every call, even a local one, is startling. The Showcase recalls these early days too, including the first railway telegraph in 1842 and the UK's first public telephone service in 1879, which had fewer than ten subscribers!

Back on St Andrew's Hill, turn left along Ireland Yard. These streets were the site of Blackfriars Monastery from the late 13th century until Henry VIII dissolved it in 1538. All that now remains is part of one wall, which you can see in Friar Square, almost immediately right off Ireland Yard. Friar Square, and Church Entry next to it, are both delightfully peaceful and secluded, and excellent spots for a picnic. As a plaque tells you, Church Entry later became the churchyard of St Ann Blackfriars.

Playhouse Yard

Ireland Yard now turns into Playhouse Yard, and this name too recalls more of the varied history of these streets. Just 40 years after the monks left, actors took up occupation, and the first of two theatres on this site opened to the public in what had formerly been the monastic dining-hall. Shakespeare's plays were almost certainly performed here (Shakespeare himself bought a house near Ireland Yard in 1613 for £140), but the theatre only survived until 1642.

Printing House Square

Playhouse Yard comes out into Blackfriars Lane. Just down to the left is Printing House Square, where *The Times* was produced from 1788 until 1974; its offices are now used by the *Observer*, which comes out each Sunday. There were printers here long before *The Times*, however. In the 17th century one unfortunate compositor left the word 'not' out of the Seventh Commandment – by accident or on purpose? – and the Stationers' Company, which controlled all publishing at the time, was heavily fined as a result.

Apothecaries' Hall Turn right from Playhouse Yard into Blackfriars Lane. Almost immediately on the right, opposite the junction with Apothecary Street, is the entrance to Apothecaries' Hall. The hall itself is closed to the public, but with luck the gateway will be open, and you can take a look at the lovely courtyard, quite cut off from the bustle outside. The hall was rebuilt after the Great Fire and survived the last war unscathed.

On the corner of Apothecary Street is the Food for Health restaurant, which provides excellent cheap non-meat meals of all kinds.

Old Bailey Now walk up Blackfriars Lane, and cross first Pilgrim Street and then Ludgate Hill, where there are good views up to St Paul's. The road opposite is Old Bailey, although that name is more usually used to refer to the Central Criminal Court at the far end, topped by the figure of Justice with scales and a sword. The present building – which has seen the trials of Dr Crippen, George Smith (the 'Brides-in-the-Bath' murderer) and Peter Sutcliffe (the 'Yorkshire Ripper') among many others – stands on the site of Newgate, London's most notorious and dreaded prison. Prisoners left here for the grim journey to the execution block at Tyburn (see walk 3) until 1783. For the next 85 years public executions took place here: notice how the road widens to accommodate the crowds.

Giltspur Street At the end of Old Bailey, cross straight over Newgate and start to make your way down Giltspur Street. But before you do so, have a free drink – though only of water – at the first Metropolitan Public Drinking Fountain, erected not far away in 1859 and moved here eight years later. A short way down Giltspur Street, at the corner of Cock Lane, you can make the acquaintance of the Golden Boy of Pie Corner, high up on a wall. This 17th-century Billy Bunter was put here to mark what is alleged to be the furthest point reached by the Great Fire, and also to provide a moral lesson by reminding citizens of the sin of gluttony – which, so some people said at the time, had been the cause of the fire.

81

Smithfield   Follow Giltspur Street round to the right, past the entrance to St Bartholomew's Hospital, founded in 1123, the oldest in London and commonly known as Bart's, and turn left. This is Smithfield, or 'Smooth Field' as it used to be known. The annual Bartholomew Fair was held here, with wrestling, fire-eating and tightrope-walking and many other entertainments, and there was also a regular cattle market. The meat market – which is now the world's largest and sells over 150,000 tonnes of meat a year – only started in 1868. Smithfield is a wholesale market, and so work begins early in the morning, when meat-buyers from supermarkets, butchers' shops and hotels come to buy their supplies. If you do come at that time of the day, make sure you keep out of the way of the porters.

Walk along Grand Avenue, which bisects the main market building, turn right and then left into Charterhouse Square. Portering is thirsty work, and on the left you pass the Smithfield Tavern, which – unusually for British pubs – is one of several open from 6.30 am onwards, although only to people who work in the market.

Charterhouse Square   Charterhouse Square has some attractive 18th-century houses and is a good place for a rest. The Charterhouse was a monastery founded in 1370; it became a private residence in the mid-16th century, then a home for male pensioners and a school. The school moved to Surrey more than a century ago, but pensioners still live in the old buildings; the new ones belong to the Medical School of Bart's Hospital.

St Bartholomew -the-Great   Walk round the square, then turn left into Hayne Street, cross Long Lane and go straight through the passage under Ye Old Red Cow pub. This emerges by the Hand and Shears, with its amazingly lurid pub sign. Go right along Middle Street and then along Cloth Fair, and turn left into Little Britain, so called because the Dukes of Britanny once had a house here. Immediately on the left is the entrance to St Bartholomew-the-Great, London's oldest church and all that remains of a monastery founded in 1123 by Rahere. Rahere, who also founded the hospital, was Henry I's court jester and experienced a vision in which St Bartholomew rescued him from a winged monster. The Butchers' Company holds its annual service here. As well as the church, the gateway itself is worth looking at, as the doorway dates from the 13th century and the half-timbered house is late Elizabethan.

Continue along Little Britain, then turn left along Bartholomew Court and past William Harvey's house. Harvey, who discovered that blood circulates round the body, was chief physician at Bart's from 1609 to 1633. Follow Bartholomew Court round and back into Little Britain again.

Postmen's Park
Now, quite suddenly, you leave medicine behind and the prevailing theme is the postal service. On the left you come to Postmen's Park, another good picnic spot. Beneath the wooden shelter at the far end of the park is a wall of plaques, each one commemorating a hero who died rescuing or helping another person. The wall was the idea of G.F. Watts, the Victorian artist, who wanted to establish a 'national memorial to heroic men and women'.

King Edward Building
On the opposite side and a little further up King Edward Street is the Post Office's King Edward Building, opened in 1829. Outside there is a statue of Rowland Hill, who founded the Penny Post. Inside you can visit the National Postal Museum, with its fine collection of British postage stamps and much other interesting philatelic material, including dies for the celebrated Penny Black. The rest of the building now houses a sorting office for London and Overseas letters and a magnificent ornate hall, in which you can buy stamps, postal orders, etc. Deep underground trundle the carriages of the unique Post Office Railway, which carries not passengers but bags and bags of mail – up to 50,000 a day – over a 10-kilometre (6½-mile) route linking six sorting offices and two mainline termini.

From the roof of the GPO's administrative headquarters opposite Guglielmo Marconi made the first public transmission of radio signals on 27 July 1896.

From the King Edward Building it is a short walk to St Paul's Precincts, where there are several good restaurants, including Oodles and Slenders, and to St Paul's Underground Station. The Museum of London is two minutes' walk away in the opposite direction.

Telecom Technology Showcase
135 Queen Victoria Street
London EC4V 4AT
Tel: 01-248 7444
Opening times: Mondays to Fridays 10.00am-5.00pm;
closed Bank Holidays

National Postal Museum
King Edward Building
King Edward Street
London EC1A 1LP
Tel: 01-432 3851; 01-606 3769
Opening times: Mondays to Thursdays
10.00am-4.30pm; Fridays 10.00am-4.00pm; closed
Bank Holidays

Museum of London
London Wall
London EC2 5HN
Tel: 01-600 3699
Opening times: Tuesdays to Saturdays
10.00am-6.00pm; Sundays 2.00-6.00pm

9   THE REGENT'S LONDON

Start: Oxford Circus
Underground: Oxford Circus
Buses: 1, 3, 6, 7, 8, 12, 13, 15, 16A, 23, 25,
        53, 73, 88, 113, 137, 159, 500

Finish: Camden Town
Underground: Camden Town
Buses: 3, 24, 29, 31, 46, 53, 74, 253

Distance: 9 kilometres (5¾ miles)

Places to sit down: Gardens, Paddington Street
                       Regent's Park

Eating places: Salt and Pepper Sandwich Bar,
                 Paddington Street
                 Tea house, Regent's Park

Lavatories: In centre of Regent Street, just north
of Oxford Circus
In Regent's Park, as shown on maps
Wellington Road, just north of roundabout
junction with Park Road

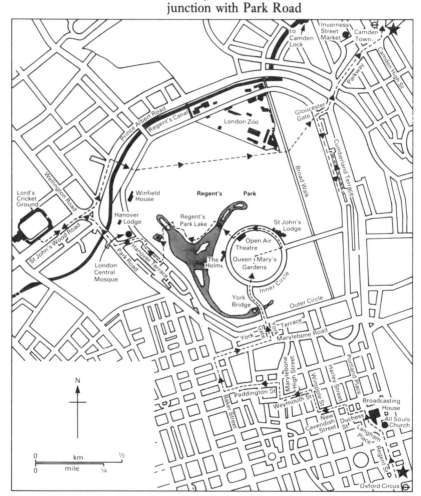

Two men dominate this walk. One is the Prince Regent,
the eldest son of George III, a man who loved great riches
and grand settings in which to display them. The other is
John Nash, architect and town-planner and intimate friend

of the Prince. In the second decade of the 19th century, the one man's wealth and power and the other's imagination and creativity came together to produce one of the most grandiose redevelopment schemes London has ever known.

The plan was to construct a sequence of grand residential and shopping streets that would link the Prince's palace at Carlton House, behind the Mall (see walk 1), and Marylebone Park, which at that time lay just to the north of the built-up area of London. The intention was to create a physical representation of the Prince's power and status. But there were other motives as well. The Crown owned Marylebone Park, and much of the land immediately north of Carlton House as well. Redevelopment of these areas would increase the value of the Crown's property and its income from rents. It would also make London look more like a true capital city: people were complaining that its cramped and narrow streets hardly fitted its status as an international capital.

Unlike many improvement schemes, by and large Nash's plans were realized. Regent Street was opened by 1819, and the park, now known as Regent's Park, was completed by 1828 – though not without a good deal of criticism of Nash's ideas, not all of which were put into practice. Ironically, by the time the builders had packed up their tools and left, so too had the Prince Regent. When he succeeded to the throne in 1820, he decided that Carlton House was no longer a palace fit for a king, and he moved to Buckingham Palace, bringing Nash in yet again to plan yet another costly remodelling.

Regent Street   The walk starts at Oxford Circus with a disappointment. The view south down Regent Street – down the Quadrant, as that stretch of Regent Street between Piccadilly and Oxford Circuses was called – is no longer of Nash's handsome colonnades, with 'shops appropriated to articles of fashion and taste' behind them. You see instead a dull and unimaginative uniform terrace of shops. The remodelling took place in the 1920s – with good reason, it seems, for the original buildings were becoming unsafe, and the shops were by then far too small for the variety of goods sold and the numbers of people who came to buy and to gaze. But what a shame it is that more notice was not taken of Nash's original design.

All Souls, Langham Place

Our route takes us in the opposite direction, north up Regent Street, past part of the Polytechnic of Central London on the left to All Souls, Langham Place. This is a lovely church, with a circular porch and above it a circular dome topped by a spikey spire that has been described as a witch's hat. The church is now used by the BBC to broadcast religious services and concerts. If you arrive at the right moment, you may hear the pure tones of the choir in rehearsal swelling out and filling the entire building.

Portland Place

Nash built All Souls to bring the northern stretch of Regent Street to a natural conclusion and to make a visual connection with Portland Place beyond. Portland Place had been built by the architect brothers Robert and James Adam, 40 years before Nash sat down at his drawing-board, and was one of the finest streets of 18th-century London. Only a few of the original houses remain, but even today you can get an idea of how elegant the original streets must have been, especially if you shut out the traffic and the parked cars from your mind's eye.

Broadcasting House

We walk up Portland Place, past Broadcasting House on the right and then turn left along Duchess Street. Broadcasting House is the headquarters of the BBC; most programmes on Radios One to Four are produced here, while the World Service comes from Bush House at Aldwych, and the BBC's television programmes come from the Televison Centre at White City in west London.

Harley Street

At the end of Duchess Street continue straight on into Mansfield Street, then turn right up Harley Street and left along New Cavendish Street. For the first 90 years or so of its life after it was built in the early 1750s, Harley Street was a fashionable place in which to live. Since the mid-19th century people of fashion have been coming here for a different reason: to be cured of their ailments (they hope). As you will see from the brass nameplates by the front doors, Harley Street is still the domain of top-price medics.

Wimpole Street Now go right into Wimpole Street and then left along Weymouth Street until you reach Marylebone High Street. All the street names around here recall the names of their original owners. Edward Harley, Earl of Oxford, had an estate at Wimpole in Cambridgeshire, married into the Portland family and was involved in developing the Portland estate in the early 18th century. Viscount Weymouth and the Cavendish family were also related to the Portlands. The poet Elizabeth Barrett lived in Wimpole Street from 1841 until her celebrated elopement with another poet, Robert Browning, in 1846.

Marylebone High Street Marylebone High Street still preserves a village atmosphere, and there are some quite ordinary shops – grocers, greengrocers and even a fishmonger – among the smart boutiques and hairdressing salons. Turn right from Weymouth Street up the High Street and then go left into Paddington Street, where the Salt and Pepper Sandwich Bar on the left is a pleasant stopping place. Alternatively you could sit outside in the attractive small gardens, which were a burial ground for much of the 18th and 19th centuries. There is a small summerhouse-like building to use if it is wet, and a lovely Victorian statue of a Street Orderly Boy.

Baker Street Continue along Paddington Street and turn right up Baker Street. The Sherlock Holmes Hotel on the right is about as near as you will come to making the acquaintance of Baker Street's most celebrated inhabitant, the enigmatic, opium-smoking solver of mysteries and conundrums. If you care to, cross Marylebone Road and make your way towards number 221B, where the great detective had his apartment – or rather, make your way to where it should be, for the entire block is occupied by the fortress-like headquarters of the Abbey National Building Society.

Marylebone Road The walk itself goes right along Marylebone Road towards the Planetarium and Madame Tussaud's. A plaque on the wall records that underneath this street was built the world's first underground railway. The line, which ran from Bishop's Road near Paddington to Farringdon Street in the City, was opened on 10 January 1863, and was operated at first by steam locomotives especially adapted to retain their smoke. (An early example of a loco used on the line is on display in the London Transport Museum; see walk 4.)

London Planetarium The Planetarium is certainly worth a visit if you are at all curious about astronomy. Its presentations are informative and entertaining; laser shows are given in the evening.

Madame Tussaud's Next door, Madame Tussaud's Waxworks is one of London's most popular tourist spots, and you are likely to find a queue no matter what time of day or year you come. Whether or not the wait is worthwhile is questionable. Madame Tussaud herself was a fascinating character. Brought up in Paris by a successful French waxwork-maker, who left her 35 of his wax figures, she spent much of her childhood in court circles, having made friends with one of the royal princesses. A few years later, during the French Revolution, she saw her childhood playmate taken to the guillotine and executed, along with many other members of the royal family and the aristocracy. For reasons that remain unclear, Madame Tussaud left France, and her husband and one of her sons, to come to England in 1802. She toured the country for many years, showing her waxworks and making wax models to commission, before opening a permanent exhibition in Baker Street in 1835.

The present exhibition consists of a large number of figures from the worlds of politics, sport, show business, royalty and so forth, and some impressive tableaux. You can see Mary Queen of Scots as she prepares for her execution, the executioner looming in the background; Queen Victoria hearing the news of her accession to the throne; the Beatles in performance; and many others. The figures are remarkably lifelike, although you sometimes wonder whether they really looked quite as they appear in wax. And then there is the Chamber of Horrors, with some faithful reconstructions of executions, including a firing squad and an all too vivid electric chair. A recent addition is a fascinating reconstruction of the Battle of Trafalgar.

Regent's Park Outside again, continue a short way along Marylebone Road and then turn left up York Gate towards Regent's

Park. Nash's and the Regent's park was not designed as a conventional park, but rather as a very early form of garden city. No less than 56 villas, each with its own substantial grounds, were to be built in the park; there would be two circuses (a circle of villas enclosing a central garden), two crescents, a lake, a canal at the northern edge, a country pavilion for the Prince; and the whole thing would be surrounded by handsome rows of terraced villas. This was the first time that anything on this scale had been planned within a city, and although not all of it was built, and not all that was built has survived, enough remains for us to realize just how grand and bold a conception it was.

York Gate leads past the end of York Terrace East and West over the Outer Circle, one of the two roads that encircle the Park, over York Bridge and alongside what used to be Bedford College, part of the University of London, but is now a Centre for Information on Language Teaching and Research. The building is quite out of keeping with Nash's style, and was erected in 1913. Then you reach the Inner Circle, which according to Nash's original plan would have been lined with terraces. There is a tea pavilion a little way along to the left.

Queen Mary's Gardens
The entrance to Queen Mary's Gardens is straight ahead. Here there is a small lake and an island with a rockery and alpine plants, a fossil wood and, most famous and lovely of all, a rose garden. The display in June is marvellous. In one corner of the gardens is the entrance to the Open Air Theatre, where there is an annual summer season of Shakespeare, plus one or two other plays. Given reasonably warm weather there can hardly be a better place in London to enjoy Shakespeare's magnificent verse.

Regent's Park Lake
Leave Queen Mary's Gardens by the east gate, and turn left along Inner Circle, past St John's Lodge, one of the eight of Nash's 56 villas that was built and one of the four that survive today. Just pass the back of the theatre – you might be able to hear lines of Shakespeare floating through the trees – turn right down the path that crosses the lake. Then go left along the lakeside and follow the path round until you reach the boat station. There are views of The Holme, another of the original Nash villas, across the lake,

of the Nash terraces on the western edge of the park and of the minaret of the London Central Mosque, which imparts an exotic flavour to the scene. The bird life is plentiful on and around the lake. Kestrel, heron, goldcrest and great crested grebe have bred here in recent years, and well over 30 species are visible in mid-summer.

Hanover Terrace At the far side of the lake make for the edge of the park, leaving the children's playground on your right. Cross Outer Circle and walk along Hanover Terrace, parallel with Outer Circle, one of Nash's more sober terraces. At the far end you will come out into Outer Circle again, but you turn left almost immediately past Little Hanover Lodge into Park Road. Hanover Lodge, another of the surviving Nash villas, is on your right, and then comes the entrance to the Islamic Cultural Centre and the London Central Mosque.

London Central Mosque The story of the mosque's construction is a long one, full of disappointments and setbacks for the Muslim community in Britain as it struggled to raise the money and obtain the permission necessary to erect the first purpose-built mosque in London. The British government donated the site as long ago as 1944; the foundation stone was laid in 1954; but the building itself was only opened in 1978, having been under construction since 1973. The main building consists of two prayer halls, one above the other. Outside the principal one, on the ground floor, are five clocks showing the five times for daily prayer. A ladies' gallery overlooks the main prayer hall at the back. Visitors are welcome to enter the prayer hall, having first removed their shoes. Visitors are asked to remain very quiet during prayer times so as not to disturb worship.

The Friday congregation attending the mosque is the largest in England. During festivals as many as 15,000 people come to worship.

The rest of the building consists of a library and reading room, offices, a residential block, and the minaret, which is 43 metres (141 feet) high and visible right across the park. The Islamic Cultural Centre does a great deal of work among the Muslim community both in London and throughout the country, organizing educational programmes, running courses and lectures, conducting marriages and divorces, and carrying out welfare work.

Lord's Cricket Ground   A short distance away, over the Regent's Canal (see walk 10) and to the left just beyond the top of Park Road, lies one of the most sacred pieces of English turf: Lord's Cricket Ground, headquarters of the Marylebone Cricket Club. Until 1970 the MCC was the governing body of English cricket but this job has now been taken over by the Cricket Council, which also meets at Lord's. On match days, of course, most people will only have eyes for the game. But at the ground there is also the Cricket Memorial Gallery, a fascinating small museum of cricket history. There is a great deal of interest here. Most notable are the Ashes, the trophy for which the English and Australian teams compete each Test series. The Ashes are quite literally that – the ashes of a cricket ball burnt by a group of disappointed Melbourne ladies in 1883, when the home team lost a series against a visiting side from England – and they are kept here permanently in a small pottery urn. The Gallery also contains many portraits and photographs of famous cricketers and teams, and bats and other equipment: colours, insignia, costumes. Also on show is a sparrow killed by a ball bowled by the Indian cricketer Jehangir Khan during a match at Lord's in 1936: the sparrow is mounted on the ball that killed him.

The Gallery is open without appointment only on match days, when you have to pay to get into the ground. An appointment to visit on a non-match day, when admission is free, can easily be made by telephoning 24 hours in advance. On non-match days a tour of the ground may also be available, and it is a visit well worth making. Standing in front of the Long Room and gazing at the famous pitch, with its quite pronounced slope, you can imagine what it must feel like to stand at the wicket, in front of a crowd of tens of thousands.

Lord's also possesses a tennis court: nothing special about that, it might be thought. This one, though, is one of the 14 real or royal tennis courts in the country. Real tennis is a much older game than the lawn variety, and was probably first played in medieval monasteries. The curious shape of the court is said to resemble a monastic cloister. With luck you may see a game in progress.

Regent's Park Leaving Lord's, retrace your steps along St John's Wood Road and carry straight on at the roundabout into Prince Albert Road, crossing Regent's Canal (see walk 10) and Outer Circle shortly to enter the park. Winfield House, the residence of the United States ambassador to Britain, is to the right. There is now a brisk walk across the park, leaving the London Zoo just to the north. Cross the Broad Walk, a shady tree-lined path that bisects the park from north to south, and make for the exit at Gloucester Gate, by a children's playground. Cumberland Terrace, a little way down Outer Circle to the right, said by many to be the most splendid of all the Nash terraces, is well worth a look. The pavilion Nash planned for the Prince Regent would have been sited opposite Cumberland Terrace, but it was never built.

Camden Town The final leg of the walk is along Parkway and into Camden Town, a lively and cosmopolitan area of north London. Camden Lock (see walk 10) is a few minutes' walk up Chalk Farm Road from the Underground Station. The Inverness Street market, on the left just beyond the station, on Wednesdays, Fridays and Saturdays has good fruit and vegetables, and other stalls there display a wide selection of junk and bric-à-brac.

London Planetarium
Marylebone Road
London NW1 5LR
Tel: 01-486 1121
Opening times: daily 11.00 am-4.30 pm 30-minute shows regularly throughout the day

Madame Tussaud's
Marylebone Road
London NW1 5LR
Tel: 01-935 6861
Opening times: daily 10.00 am-5.30 pm

Islamic Cultural Centre

146 Park Road
London NW8 7RG
Tel: 01-724 3363-7
Opening times: The Mosque is open throughout
the year for prayer. Guided tours are also available;
apply in advance for an appointment.

Cricket Memorial Gallery

Lord's Ground
London NW8 8QN
Tel: 01-289 1611
Opening times: On match days, Mondays to
Saturdays 10.30 am-5.00 pm; on other days by prior
appointment only (telephone 24 hours in advance)

London Zoo

Outer Circle
Regent's Park
London NW1 4RY
Tel: 01-722 3333
Opening times: 1 March to 31 October: Mondays to
Saturdays 9.00 am-6.00 pm or dusk (whichever is earlier);
Sundays and Bank Holidays 9.00 am-7.00 pm;
1 November to 28 February: daily 10.00 am-dusk

10 THE REGENT'S CANAL

Start: Little Venice, Blomfield Road
Underground: Warwick Avenue
Buses: 6, 8, 16, 16A, 176

Finish: Camden Lock
Underground: Camden Town, Chalk Farm
Buses: 3, 24, 27, 29, 31, 53, 68, 74, 134, 137, 214, 253
or
Finish: Islington Tunnel, Muriel Street
Underground: Angel
Buses: 4, 19, 30, 38, 43, 73, 104, 153, 171, 214, 277,
      279, 279A (from Angel)
      14, 45, 221, 259 (from Caledonian Road)

Distance: Little Venice to Camden Lock
      4·8 kilometres (3 miles)
      Camden Lock to Islington Tunnel
      2·4 kilometres (1½ miles)

Places to sit down: More or less anywhere along
the towpath

Eating places: Huffs, 28 Chalk Farm Road
Marine Ices, 8 Haverstock Hill

There are many contrasts between 19th-and 20th-century
London. But you will hardly find a greater or a more vivid
one than along the Regent's Canal.

Walk today along the 14-kilometre (8½-mile) towpath
between Little Venice in the west and the Thames at
Limehouse in the east, and, except at one or two popular
tourist spots, you will scarcely meet another person; only a
few narrow boats or motor launches will pass you.
Normally, the ducks and the moorhens and the occasional
swans have the canal to themselves, and you will be hard
put to believe that you are virtually in the heart of London,
just a few kilometres away from the grand shops and hotels
and office blocks.

If we could return to the 19th century, however – to any
year after 1820, when the canal was opened – the scene
would be quite different. The water then was busy with
narrow boats, often pulling a butty (a smaller subsidiary
barge) behind them. Their cargoes were coal, or timber, or
tiles, or grain, or any of the 101 other things that the
expanding capital city needed from the farms and factories
and mines of the Midlands and North. Boats travelling in
the other direction, out of London, were equally laden,
perhaps with materials and spices brought into London's
docks from overseas. In the early years of the canal the
brightly painted narrow boats were pulled by horses
tramping along the towpath, although by the 1860s steam
boats were being introduced, and the air was thick with the
smoke – and the smell – of burning coke.

Canals were the first of Britain's three transport
revolutions. Before the first canal was built, by the Duke of
Bridgewater near Manchester in 1761, footpower and
horsepower were virtually the only means of travel. Unless
you happened to live near a river, and wanted to go where
that river flowed, you either walked or rode, on horseback
or in a stagecoach. Goods were carried the same way. As a

97

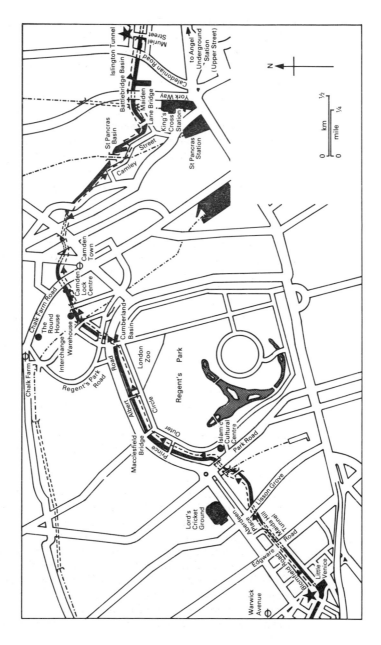

result only the rich travelled much, and there was relatively little trade between different parts of the country.

The construction of a national canal network changed all that. Not only was it easier for people to get about, but raw materials or manufactured goods from one part of the country could be sold in another area tens or even hundreds of kilometres away – and relatively cheaply too, for canal transport was not expensive.

Although the second transport revolution – the railways – came hard on the heels of the canals (the first lines were built in the 1830s, just as the canal network was being completed), the two forms of transport did not immediately become rivals. For much of the 19th century both the railway and the canal were used to carry freight and often, as happened on the Regent's Canal, goods would travel on both rail and water during their journey from factory to shop. (However, railways did soon take over most of the canals' passenger-carrying business.)

Canals continued to carry quite substantial amounts of freight, particularly heavy, bulky goods such as coal, timber and minerals, until well into the 1930s. It was only the third transport revolution – the development of motor transport, particularly of heavy lorries – that put paid to canals as working routes. After the Second World War freight traffic on canals decreased dramatically and by the 1960s it had virtually died out.

Following a dismal period in which there seemed to be no future for the canals, in the last 20 years or so they have experiencd a remarkable revival, as more and more people have taken to canal boats for holidays and weekends and days out. Walkers and fishermen have also discovered the delights of the canals.

All this may seem a rather lengthy preamble to a walk along the Regent's Canal, but knowing something of how canals developed nationally helps to fit the Regent's Canal into the picture. The first canal in London was built quite late in the canal age, in 1794, when the Grand Junction Canal was opened between Brentford, on the north bank of the Thames opposite Kew, and Braunston, in Northamptonshire, 150 kilometres (93 miles) to the north. The Grand Junction was so called because it linked the Thames – and hence the capital city and its expanding docks – with the growing canal network that served many of the new industrial centres in the Midlands and the North. Seven years later a branch of the Grand Junction was opened to Paddington. This brought canal traffic almost to the heart of the city, and factories with their own wharves were soon built along the canal banks.

Nineteen more years passed, and numerous complications had to be overcome, before the Regent's Canal was opened. Barges now had a direct route to the docks and also to places such as Camden Town and Islington, which were at that time on the edges of the built-up area, where new factories and workshops were springing up. Nowadays, confusingly, the entire canal route from the Thames to the Midlands is known as the Grand Union.

The canal takes its name from the Prince Regent. An early plan, put forward by one Thomas Homer, had been to drive the new waterway straight through central London. However, even in those days land was costly, and the idea was abandoned. Homer then came up with a more northerly route, and enlisted the support of the architect John Nash, a close associate of the Prince Regent. Nash was then working on his grand scheme to link Marylebone Park (later re-named Regent's Park) to the Regent's palace at Carlton House via a grand new shopping and residential street (see walks 1 and 9). Nash liked the idea of the canal, and originally planned it to run through the centre of the park. But the authorities opposed that idea – canal people and their horses and dogs were rough and would spoil the genteel atmosphere of the park – and he was forced to accept a route along its northern edge.

Nowadays you can walk the entire length of the canal. The most interesting stretches are from Little Venice to Camden Lock, and then on to Islington Tunnel.

Little Venice Little Venice is a comparatively recent name for what was formerly – and more prosaically – called Paddington Basin. It was here that the Paddington arm of the Grand Junction terminated. Nowadays, instead of working canal boats, it is pleasure craft that tie up here, and you can take waterbuses that will convey you – at a very sedate pace – west towards Uxbridge or east along the Regent's Canal to London Zoo and Camden Lock. A small colony of canal houseboats is moored here.

Maida Hill Tunnel   Above the canal are some fine streets of elegant town houses built by Nash. Then comes an attractive canalside cottage called Junction House, followed by the mouth of the Maida Hill Tunnel, 249 metres (272 yards) long and the first of the two tunnels on the Regent's Canal. In the days of horsedrawn boats, one of the crew walked the horse over the top of the tunnel, while the rest 'legged' the boats through it. In the 19th century and well into the 20th, boat families operated the canal craft. They were isolated, self-sufficient people who passed their skills and knowledge on from one generation to the next and rarely had much contact with anyone outside the canal community.

Through London by Canal, an account of the Regent's Canal written in 1885, gives a good description of legging a boat through the Maida Hill Tunnel:

'Two long planks are hinged together in the middle so that they are folded up and laid away, and when unfolded and hooked on to irons fitted for that purpose the wings project on each side near the bow nearly to the sides of the tunnel. On each wing a man lies flat on his back – an extra man is waiting here to be taken on for such work –and these tread slantingly with their feet along the wall, thus painfully propelling the boat.'

The walker's route above the tunnel is straightforward: along Blomfield Road, across Edgware Road, along Aberdeen Place, then along the footpath beside the canal railings and out into Lisson Grove. Cross the road here to the steps that head down to the canal bank again. The Lisson Grove housing estate was built on the site of the old Marylebone goodsyard.

The canal now passes under two railway bridges and a road bridge. The railway bridges carry the Metropolitan lines from Baker Street to Harrow and Amersham (strictly speaking the Underground, although the trains run overground for almost the entire journey) and the British Rail commuter services from Marylebone to Aylesbury and Banbury. The steps by the road bridge lead up to Park Road, a short walk from Lord's Cricket Ground, the

Cricket Memorial Gallery and the Islamic Cultural Centre (see walk 9).

Blow-up Bridge   The next bridge but one, officially called Macclesfield Bridge, is more often known as Blow-up Bridge. The nickname comes from an explosion in the small hours of 10 October 1874, when five tonnes of gunpowder on board one of a string of barges caught fire. The crew of four was killed, nearby houses were severely damaged and windows were blown out of buildings over a considerable area. The supporting columns of the bridge were retrieved from the rubble, and used again when the bridge was rebuilt – but the reverse way round, as you can see when you look closely, for grooves made by the canal horses' towing ropes appear on both sides.

London Zoo   The canal now runs along the edge of Regent's Park, alongside London Zoo, and you get a good view of some of the zoo's inhabitants – as they likewise do of you. The magnificent airy aviary designed by Lord Snowdon is on your left.

Railways   Past the zoo the towpath bends left past Cumberland Basin, which originally led to Cumberland Market, where hay and straw were sold during the 19th century. The next bridge but one carries the main line north out of Euston station. This was the first long-distance main line from London. For the first few years locomotives were not powerful enough to tackle the steep incline between Euston and Camden Town, just to the north, and the carriages had to be hauled up the slope of a fixed winding cable. The castle immediately ahead on the right is a piece of contemporary fantasy built in 1977 for a youth club. Its architect, Richard Seifert, is better known for rather more stark and bold work, in particular Centre Point, the tall office block at the corner of Tottenham Court Road and Charing Cross Road. The small electricity power station opposite Pirates' Castle has been built in the same style.

As well as building a magnificent terminus at Euston (now sadly replaced by a modern structure) for their London & Birmingham Railway, the Stephensons, George and Robert, father and son, built a large goodsyard immediately behind the canal to the north with warehouses and stables. Many of these survive today, in what is one of the most interesting and accessible collections of industrial buildings in London.

Interchange Warehouse The first, the Interchange Warehouse, is immediately on the left past the power station. The towpath runs over a small bridge, and if you look down you will see that an inlet of the canal branches underneath the building itself. Freight wagons entered the warehouse from the sidings at high level, barges entered by water from below, and goods were transferred directly from one to the other. The upper floors, which are lit from above, were used for storage.

Stables Go through Camden Lock Centre (see below), follow Chalk Farm Road a little way north under the railway bridge, and you will come to a large group of stables and warehouses to the left of the road. Stables were a vital part of any 19th-century goodsyard, for it was horses then that distributed the goods over a wide area. The first stables here were built in 1855. These housed horses at ground level and had hay lofts above. New blocks were added in the 1880s and 1890s, so that by the end of the century there was accommodation for more than 420 horses. You can see the ramps along which they were led to the stables on the upper floors, and inside some of the stables the original fittings are preserved almost intact.

Camden Lock Back at the canal there is a lovely iron roving bridge and at its foot, on the lock side, a winch brought here from the Regent's Canal Dock at Limehouse, where it was used to close lock gates. The vertical part of the lock-keeper's cottage is original.

Camden Lock Centre Camden Lock Centre, which has restaurants, craft shops and studios and, at weekends, a very popular and crowded market, is built on the site of Dingwall's Timber Wharf and Dock. The sense of hubbub and fun spills out on to the main road, and it is easy to spend a pleasant couple of hours looking at the shops and stalls and drinking in the atmosphere. There is a pleasant restaurant called Huffs in Chalk Farm Road, and Marine Ices – one of London's best ice cream parlours – is ten minutes' gentle stroll north up Chalk Farm Road. The ices are delicious and quite cheap if you buy a cone to take away. Opposite Marine Ices is another rare railway building, the Round House. Constructed in 1847 to accommodate a locomotive turntable, it was later used as a warehouse and a factory and, since 1960, as a theatre and arts centre.

The walk east along the canal to Islington Tunnel runs past the jazzy new studios of TV-AM, past two more locks (there are 12 in all between Camden Lock and the Thames, falling a total of 26 metres/86 feet) and under a number of bridges to St Pancras Basin. The atmosphere on this stretch of the canal is quite different. Gone is the country-like feeling of Regent's Park, and gone too are the well-tended gardens stretching down to the water's edge from elegant, expensive canalside homes. This is – or rather was – industrial London, and now that most of the factories have closed or moved away much of the land is derelict.

Camley Street Natural Park Just before St Pancras Basin, and on the opposite side of the canal from the towpath, lies Camley Street Natural Park. The park is a fascinating place, and worth the long detour from the canal if you want to see the amazing variety of wildlife that a small piece of the inner city can support. There is a large pond, reedbeds and marshy areas, meadow areas around the pond, and scrubland around the edge of the park. Many different species of plants, animals, insects and birds can be seen.

St Pancras Basin The canal now passes under the railway lines leading into St Pancras Station, which was built by the Midland Railway in 1867, and you get an excellent view of the splendid glass and iron train shed. It is 210 metres (689 feet) long, 30 metres (100 feet) above the rails at its highest point, and has a span of 73 metres (240 feet). Here you are in St Pancras Basin, where there is another lock. Beyond there is a view into another railway terminus, King's Cross, built a little earlier in 1852 by the Great Northern Railway. There are two train sheds, each simple and functional. The lines out of King's Cross run under the canal, and were often flooded in the early years; hence the Midland's decision to go over the water.

Islington Tunnel The final stretch to Islington Tunnel runs under Maiden Lane Bridge, past Battlebridge Basin and alongside council flats. The mouth of the tunnel looms ahead, and even today the sight of a boat coming towards you, visible only by the beam of its lamp, can be slightly eerie. As at Maida Hill, boats were legged through the 880-metre (960-yard) tunnel, while the horse made its way over the hill.

The walk ends here, although you can continue along the towpath through Hackney and Mile End to Salmon Lane Lock in Limehouse, which brings the canal into Limehouse Basin, the meeting-place with the Thames.

On top of the hill, in and around Upper Street, there are interesting shops and markets. Chapel Market, which operates daily except on Mondays and on Thursday and Saturday afternoons, has food and cheap clothing and household goods. Camden Passage, on the other side of the main road, is a complete contrast, selling only rather pricey antiques and bric-à-brac every Wednesday and Saturday.

Camley Street Natural Park

Camley Street
London NW1
Tel: 01-833 2311
Opening times: Mondays to Fridays and alternate weekends 10.00 am-5.30 pm; it is advisable to check opening times by telephone

Boat trips are run by the following organizations:

Jason's Trip

60 Blomfield Road
London W9
Tel: 01-286 3424

Jenny Wren Cruises

250 Camden High Street
London NW1
Tel: 01-485 4435

London Waterbus Company

Camden Lock
London NW1
Tel: 01-485 2550

11   DOWN THE THAMES

Boats leave Westminster Pier every 20 minutes
between 10.00am and 5.00pm, and Charing Cross
Pier every 30 minutes between 10.30am and 4.30pm.
Boats from Charing Cross call at the Festival Pier
5 minutes later. All boats call at Tower Pier.

Westminster Pier
Underground: Westminster
Buses: 3, 11, 12, 24, 29, 53, 70, 76, 77, 77A, 88,
        109, 159, 170, 184

Charing Cross Pier
Underground: Embankment
Buses: 1, 1A, 3, 6, 9, 11, 12, 13, 15, 23, 24, 53, 77,
        77A, 88, 159, 170, 173 (at Trafalgar Square)

Festival Pier

Underground: Waterloo
Buses: 1, 1A, 4, 5, 68, 70, 76, 149, 155, 171,
176, 177, 188, 501, 502, 507, 513
(at south end of Waterloo Bridge)
12, 53, 70, 76, 77, 109, 149, 155, 159, 170, 171,
184, 507 (at south end of Westminster Bridge)

Greenwich

BR train: from Maze Hill or Greenwich to London
Bridge, Waterloo East and Charing Cross
Buses: 108B, 177, 180, 185, 188

For up-to-date information, and to check times, contact
the London Visitor & Convention Bureau's riverboat
information service: Tel: 01-730 4812.
The trip from central London to Greenwich takes
approximately 1 hour.

The Thames is London's neglected highway. For centuries
it was one of the principal thoroughfares, and was quite as
busy as any street on land. Watermen carried Londoners
from one bank to the other on their boats, and up and
downstream between the City and Westminster. Ships
docked in the heart of the city. There were splendid royal
processions as the monarch sailed downstream from
Hampton Court Palace or embarked at Westminster for
Greenwich. In cold winters, when the river froze, there
was even skating, and oxen were roasted on the ice.

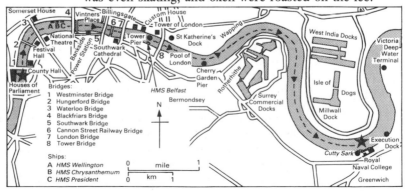

The Start Trips downstream to Greenwich start either at Westminster Pier, just downstream of Westminster Bridge; or from Charing Cross Pier, on the Embank ment just downstream of Hungerford Bridge. Boats from Charing Cross also call at the Festival Pier, on the south bank in front of the Festival Hall, and there is an intermediate stop at Tower Pier, in front of the Tower of London.

The boat pulls away from Westminster Pier and positions itself in mid-stream. On the right is County Hall, at the time of writing still the headquarters of the Greater London Council. The GLC runs many Londonwide services and is the overall planning authority for the capital; what will happen to County Hall when the GLC is abolished in May 1986 is not yet certain. On the left is the Ministry of Defence (see walk 2) and then two floating drinking places, the *PS Tattershall Castle,* which formerly saw service as a ferry across the river Humber, and the *Hispaniola.*

Bridges and Tunnels We pass first under Hungerford Bridge. As well as the eight bridges between Westminster and Greenwich, there are eight tunnels running under this stretch of the Thames. Five of these carry Underground lines (the Bakerloo, two branches of the Northern, the Waterloo & City and the East London line); one, the Tower Subway, was originally a foot tunnel and now carries services (see walk 6); the Rotherhithe Tunnel is for road traffic; and finally, at Greenwich, there is the pedestrian tunnel across to the Isle of Dogs.

Hungerford Bridge Hungerford Bridge was opened in 1864 to carry the railway across to the new Charing Cross Station. The bridge takes its name from Hungerford Market, on the site of which the station was built. On the left, but now some way inshore since the Victoria Embankment was completed in 1870, is the York Watergate (see walk 4) and then, on the water's edge, Cleopatra's Needle. To the right is the South Bank arts centre, which consists of three concert halls, including the well-known Festival Hall (so called because the Festival of Britain in 1951 was held on this part of the riverfront), an art gallery (the Hayward Gallery), the National Film Theatre and, beyond Waterloo

Bridge, the National Theatre, now successfully ensconced in its new home.

National Theatre The rather forbidding concrete exterior of the National hides an extremely comfortable interior. Its creation became a long-running drama in its own right. The idea of a national theatre company was first put forward as long ago as 1848. It took endless argument, and the laying of at least four foundation stones on different sites, before the company finally got going in 1962, and it was another 14 years after that when the present building opened.

Next to the National is a new building designed for IBM by Denys Lasdun, who also built the National Theatre. The buildings next to that are the headquarters of London Weekend Television, which is on the air from Friday evenings until Sunday nights, and the Oxo warehouse, built in 1928.

Waterloo Bridge The present Waterloo Bridge was built between 1938 and 1942 to replace an earlier bridge dating from 1817. The view from the bridge is magnificent, with the Houses of Parliament in one direction, and St Paul's and the City in the other.

Somerset House Immediately on the left past Waterloo Bridge is Somerset House. The present building, now the headquarters of the Inland Revenue, dates from the late 18th century. Its predecessor had been built in the 1540s for Lord Protector Somerset, and had chiefly been used as a royal palace. King's College, part of the University of London, and the manicured lawns of the Inner Temple Garden (see walk 5) now come into view on the left. The boats moored downstream of Temple Steps, which mark the boundary between Westminster and the City, are *HMS Wellington*, *HMS Chrysanthemum* and *HMS President*. *Wellington*, a sloop, is the hall of the Honourable Company of Master Mariners (walk 7 describes the history of City Livery Companies); and *Chrysanthemum* and *President* are used by the Royal Naval Reserve.

Blackfriars Bridge Beyond the two Blackfriars bridges, the first a road bridge (built in the 1760s and replaced a century later), the second carrying the railway (built in the 1880s), you begin to sense a gradual change of atmosphere. This is the river that Londoners knew not only 500 years ago, but nearly 2,000 years back, when the Romans built their first settlements here. Queenhithe Dock on the north bank has been in operation for at least 800 years. (We can be sure that many Londoners visited it, for the City's first public lavatory was here.) Just beyond it is Vintners Place, where the Vintners' Company has its hall. The Vintners, together with the Crown and the Dyers' Company, own all the swans on the Thames. Sadly, recent development has destroyed much of the atmosphere of the quays and riverside here. The Fleet river, now merely a sewer, flows into the Thames just downstream of Blackfriars Bridge.

The south bank between Blackfriars Bridge and Tower Bridge is described in detail in walk 6.

Southwark Bridge The first Southwark Bridge was opened in 1819; it was replaced by the present one in 1921. It is followed almost immediately by Cannon Street Railway Bridge, with its well-known twin towers, built in the 1860s and widened 25 years later. Nowadays Cannon Street is chiefly a commuter station with services to south-east London and Kent.

London Bridge Ahead now is London Bridge, the capital's first and most famous bridge, and for a long time its only road crossing. The present structure is the third built of stone, and these three were preceded by at least another three – perhaps more, no one can say for certain – built of wood. *The* London Bridge – the one that everyone mentally pictures falling down – was one of the early wooden structures. The 'falling down' was in 1014, when King Ethelred burnt the bridge as a defensive measure against a force of Danish raiders. The event immediately caught the public imagination, and has remained there ever since, although the current version of the nursery rhyme only dates back as far as the mid-17th century.

For many centuries London Bridge was a centre of hustle and bustle, as people crossed to and from Southwark, and travellers from Kent and the Continent urged their horses over the final stretch of a long journey. In times of revolt the drawbridge (which was on the south

111

side) was pulled up, and access to the City denied the rebels; usually not for long, though, for as soon as the rebels threatened to burn the bridge the authorities would let them across. For several hundred years it was the practice to par-boil the severed heads of traitors, then dip them in tar to preserve them, and finally hoist them above the gatehouse.

The first stone London Bridge, which lasted from 1176 to 1831, looked quite different from today's sleek but uninspiring structure. It was lined with houses up to seven storeys high, and had shops (in 1358 no less than 138 of them) and a chapel. The houses were demolished between 1758 and 1762. There were 19 arches which, together with wooden platforms known as starlings around the foot of each pier, channelled the water into a turbulent and extremely dangerous current. In hard winters those arches caused the river to ice over.

The second stone London Bridge was erected in 1831 and dismantled 140 years later – whereupon it was sold, lock, stock and stone, and re-erected just as it was in Lake Havasu City, Arizona, USA.

Pool of London

Beyond London Bridge we enter the Pool of London, strictly speaking the Upper Pool, which is the name for the stretch of river between Cherry Garden Pier (see below) and London Bridge. Until the enclosed docks were built in the early 19th century (see walk 6), vessels of every description packed this part of the river, and lighters ferried goods to and from the warehouses on the river bank.

On the north bank we pass Billingsgate, the site of the capital's wholesale fish market from at least the 13th century until 1982. The market now occupies modern premises on the Isle of Dogs further downstream and the Victorian building here is being redeveloped. Downstream of the market is the Custom House with its long waterfront, where you are almost certain to see at least one customs vessel tied up. Customs and Excise officials have been working from here for more than seven centuries and still ensure that the correct duties are paid on goods entering the country. The present Custom House dates from 1817, although part of it collapsed eight years later and had to be rebuilt; the architect got the sack.

Tower of London Now we can see the Tower of London. Imagine how massive and imposing it must have seemed to Londoners in the Middle Ages when, along with St Paul's Cathedral, it dominated the capital's skyline: a visible reminder of the power of the monarch. How many prisoners passed from the river – perhaps they came by the route we have just taken – through Traitor's Gate and on to the darkness of the dungeons and the finality of the execution block?

London's Docks Midstream above Tower Bridge lies *HMS Belfast*, described in walk 6. Beyond Tower Bridge, the last bridge before the sea, and St Katharine's Dock (see walk 6), the skyline changes. The London familiar to visitors is left behind, and the Thames appears very much a working river. And so it was until about the mid-1960s, with the Surrey Docks on the south bank and the West India and Millwall Docks on the north busy with vessels from almost every part of the globe.

Why then is the Thames so deserted nowadays, and why has Tilbury, far downstream near the mouth of the Thames, taken over as London's principal port? One reason is the size of modern ships, which are too large to travel far upstream. Another is the development of containers, in which these days the majority of goods are shipped. Containers need large amounts of storage space, which is unavailable in the built-up areas. Yet another reason for the change is distribution: roads in London are narrow and crowded, and it is quicker (and therefore cheaper) for lorries to make straight for Tilbury and the other commercial ports around the south-east coast.

Thames Vessels That said, you will be very unlucky indeed if you fail to see some craft during the trip down to Greenwich. About 330 dumb barges operate on the Thames in London, and there are also a hundred self-propelled barges. The dumb barges (the term simply signifies that they are unpowered) are towed in strings behind a tug, and carry bulk goods of all kinds – scrap metal, building materials, timber, pulp and paper – up- and downstream, often to connect with oceangoing vessels berthed at Tilbury. From the Victoria Deep Water Terminal, on the north bank about two-thirds of the way down to Greenwich from Tower Bridge, container ships and general cargo vessels regularly leave for Bulgaria and countries round the Mediterranean. There are also short sea-crossings to Rotterdam, to make connections with large oceangoing vessels in the port there.

The other product (if that is the correct word) that you may well see is waste. Until recently much of London's rubbish – and there is an awful lot of it, about 3.5 million tonnes a year – used to be carried down the Thames away from the capital in tarpaulin-covered barges. Inevitably some of it got spilt, which led to problems of pollution. Now, as a result of a GLC scheme, much of it will travel either in brand-new roller-shutter barges or in containers on board specially constructed giant 500-tonne barges. Its destination is waste land on the banks of the Thames in Essex, where heavy compactor vehicles compress it into the ground. One of these landfill sites is aptly named Mucking.

River Police Other vessels you may see include the *London Phoenix*, the London Fire Brigade's new fireboat, and the boats of the Thames Division, Metropolitan Police, whose Divisional Headquarters are on the north bank of the Thames at Wapping, a short distance beyond Tower Bridge. Thames Division is responsible for some 87 kilometres (54 miles) of river, and its 145 officers and men work from four police stations, at Wapping, at Waterloo Pier and much further upstream at Barnes and Shepperton. Much of their work is the same as police work everywhere, and, like their colleagues on land, Thames Division men go out to patrol a beat. The difference is that instead of panda cars they use boats and launches. As well as protecting life and property on the river, the Division also has to deal with vessels that have collided, fires on board ship or on the riverfront, property salvage and drifting barges. They must also deal with any dead bodies found floating in the river (some 60 or 70 a year at the last count).

Cherry Garden Pier Beyond St Katharine's Dock the first landmark on the right is Cherry Garden Pier, which in the 17th century led to Cherry Gardens, a popular pleasure garden. Ships that require Tower Bridge to be opened so that they can pass through sound their hooters here as a signal to the Bridgemaster. On the left are Execution Dock, where pirates and other criminals were hanged and their bodies left to sway and putrefy in the wind, and Oliver's Wharf. This massive warehouse, once used to store timber, has now been converted into luxury riverside flats that sell for very high prices.

Thames Tunnel Below the riverbed here runs the Thames Tunnel, the first underwater tunnel in the world. Marc Brunel, father of the celebrated engineer Isambard Kingdom Brunel and a distinguished engineer in his own right, was in charge of its construction. He invented a new method of tunnelling with a shield: only a few centimetres of earth were excavated at a time, which minimized the risk of the tunnel falling in. Nevertheless, it did collapse at least five times, and a number of workers were drowned. The tunnel, which took 20 years to complete and was opened in 1843, was used as a pedestrian route until the 1860s, when it became part of the East London Railway. Underground trains on the line from Whitechapel to New Cross and New Cross Gates still use it.

Rotherhithe Rotherhithe on the south bank still has a village atmosphere with some elegant houses grouped round the church and the Mayflower pub, named after the *Mayflower* which moored near here before she set sail carrying the Pilgrim Fathers to America. The first basin of the enclosed Surrey Commercial Docks was built here in the early 19th century. Eventually, after extensions throughout the century, there were nine docks and six timber ponds (the principal cargo handled was timber) and the whole complex covered 48 hectares (120 acres). Until recently some of the grand storage sheds remained, but these have now been demolished and small factories and houses are springing up in their place. Near the now derelict entrance to the docks a small dome marks the pedestrian access to the Rotherhithe Tunnel, which runs beneath the river here.

More or less opposite on the left bank is the Prospect of Whitby, one of the best-known riverside pubs. The

Prospect was a ship from Whitby that moored alongside the inn.

West India Docks As the river bends south, the boat passes the entrance to the Regent's Canal on the left. The history of the canal is explained in walk 10. Beyond it on the same side of the river is the entrance to West India Docks, which cross the neck of the Isle of Dogs. Opened in 1802, these were the first enclosed docks built beside the Thames. Ships entered and left by the eastern entrance, while lighters, which carried goods further upstream, came in at the western end, so avoiding congestion. Incoming and outgoing vessels were also handled in different docks. Previously it had taken four weeks to discharge ships moored in the Thames itself; now this time was reduced to four days. Goods could be stored in the 1.2 kilometres (¾ mile) of continuous warehouses five storeys high built alongside the dock. Some way beyond is the entrance to Millwall Dock, which opened in 1868.

The end of the journey is now in sight, and there are good
views of the Greenwich Observatory and the Park, with the masts of the *Cutty Sark* standing out above the buildings.

On the south bank a large housing estate with tower blocks occupies the site of the Royal Dock, or King's Yard, and the Royal Victoria Victualling Yard. Henry VIII built the Royal Dock for the construction and upkeep of his navy. Vast stores – of sugar, rum, ships' biscuits (baked in a bakery in the yard) and everything else required for a long voyage – were maintained here. The attractive officers' houses and warehouses facing the river were built in the late 18th century and are now part of the estate. Samuel Pepys, the celebrated diarist, often travelled downstream to inspect the yard when he was Secretary of the Navy. It was here too in 1581 that Elizabeth I knighted Francis Drake after his circumnavigation of the globe in the *Golden Hind.*

Great Eastern Another famous vessel was built on the opposite bank: Isambard Kingdom Brunel's *Great Eastern.* No less than 207 metres (680 feet) long, she was the longest vessel built in the country until the 1890s. Several attempts to launch her had to be made before she finally entered the water on

30 January 1858. The strain of building the *Great Eastern*, and the many setbacks he encountered, ruined Brunel's health and his finances.

Greenwich The fine buildings of the Royal Naval College are now in sight, and the journey ends at Greenwich, where a pleasant day can be spent (see walk 12). Beyond Greenwich the river flows on past Woolwich and the Thames Barrier, a magnificent piece of engineering built to prevent the river from bursting its banks and flooding much of London, on again to Dartford, to the docks at Tilbury, past Southend to the North Sea – and so to the wider world beyond the horizon.

12   GREENWICH

Start: Greenwich Pier
By boat from Westminster, Charing Cross, Festival
and Tower Piers. Boats leave Westminster Pier at
roughly 20-minute intervals between 10.00 am and
5.00 pm, and Charing Cross Pier about every half-
hour between 10.30 pm and 4.30 pm.
Boats from Charing Cross also call at the Festival
Pier by the Festival Hall. All boats stop at Tower Pier
en route.
By British Rail from Charing Cross, Waterloo East or
London Bridge stations to Greenwich or Maze Hill.

Buses: 108B, 177, 180, 185, 188

Distance: River walk: 1·6 kilometres (1 mile)
Park Walk: 3·2 kilometres (2 miles)

Places to sit down: On riverfront by the Royal Naval
College. In Greenwich Park

Eating places: MacDonalds, King William Walk
(*not* the chain)
Tea House, Greenwich Park

Lavatories: At ferry terminal
At corner of King William Walk
and Nelson Road

Even though it is so near central London (famous landmarks such as the Post Office Tower and St Paul's are visible from the top of Greenwich Park), there is something quite different about Greenwich. A sense of adventure, of a wider world beyond London, hangs in the air. Partly it is the presence of the *Cutty Sark* and *Gipsy Moth IV,* both of which have seen daring exploits. Partly it is the river itself, which carries more traffic here and has something of the feel of the sea.

Greenwich is an excellent place for a day out. As well as the ships and the museums, there are interesting shops and markets, and a fine river walk, while the park is a good place to relax and play in the sun.

If you come by train, you will travel on the first railway line built in London, along a 6-kilometre (3¾-mile) viaduct starting at London Bridge. But the river approach is without question the best. From quite far off the rigging of the *Cutty Sark* can be glimpsed. Then your boat rounds a bend and you confront the full majesty of the riverfront, the imposing buildings of the Royal Naval College leading the eye back to the Queen's House behind and then up the hill to the Royal Observatory.

Greenwich has been a royal place for many centuries. Three celebrated monarchs – Henry VIII, Mary and Elizabeth I – were born here, and Henry VIII married two of his unfortunate wives here. It was probably at Greenwich too that Sir Walter Raleigh cast down his cloak for Elizabeth – if indeed that famous incident ever happened at all.

Greenwich's present appearance dates from the early 17th century, when Anne of Denmark, James I's wife, started to build the Queen's House as a country retreat (it was only completed after her death). Later in the century

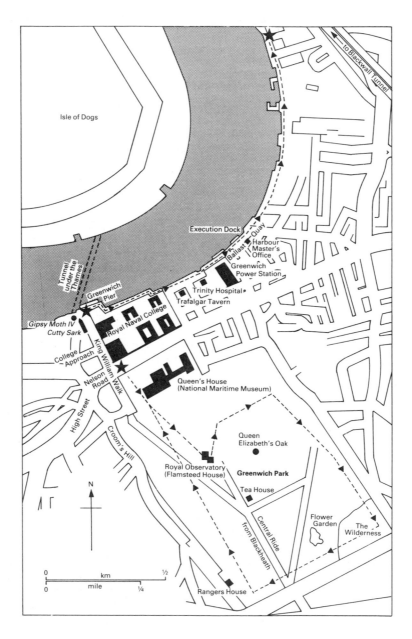

Charles II decided to rebuild the old palace on the riverside, but after five years, when just one wing was built, he ran out of money. The project got under way again in 1692 at Queen Mary's instigation, not as a royal palace (Kensington Palace, see walk 3, was by then the favourite royal home) but as a Naval Hospital, and this in turn became the Royal Naval College in 1873.

Gipsy Moth IV The first stop after you leave Greenwich Pier is *Gipsy Moth IV*. It hardly seems possible that one man alone sailed this vessel, only 16 metres (54 feet) long, around the globe and achieved the fastest single-handed circumnavigation ever. Francis Chichester left Plymouth on 27 August 1966 and returned there 229 days later, having sailed 47,685 kilometres (29,630 miles), broken by only a single brief stop on dry land in Sydney, Australia. The voyage demanded incredible tenacity and toughness, never more so than in the passage around Cape Horn, at the southern tip of South America, one of the most difficult sea passages in the world.

Six weeks after reaching Plymouth, Chichester sailed up the Thames to Greenwich. Waiting there, in front of a large crowd, was the Queen, who knighted him on the riverside by the Royal Naval College with the same sword that her namesake Elizabeth I had used 400 years before to honour Sir Francis Drake (see walk 11).

Inside, *Gipsy Moth* seems remarkably spacious. You can see the self-steering apparatus, without which any long solo voyage would be impossible. The domestic details are fascinating: the champagne set aside for Chichester's 65th birthday at sea; the mustard and cress grown for extra vitamins; the gimballed chair in which Chichester ate and worked, designed to counteract the movement of the boat. The maritime charts Chichester used are on display, and you can trace his route on them. Outside, notice how the boat is built long and narrow for speed.

Cutty Sark One of the world's last great sailing ships towers over *Gipsy Moth. Cutty Sark* is a clipper, built originally to bring tea from China to England. It was the Americans who developed the clipper style in the 19th century: narrow, sharp vessels, with stepped masts and a huge expanse of sail, that could really race through the water. Faced with competition from the American clippers, the British soon had to follow suit, and *Cutty Sark* was built in 1869. But by then it was too late. The Suez Canal, which only steamships could navigate, was opened the same year, and fast as they were (the *Cutty Sark* could cover 580 kilometres/360 miles a day) the clippers could not compete on the longer route round Africa. *Cutty Sark* was switched to the Australian wool run, where she gave magnificent service, soundly defeating her rival clipper *Thermopylae* in several races to England. Eventually, though, steam replaced sail on that route too, and *Cutty Sark* was sold to a Portuguese concern, which sailed her all over the world until 1922, when she was returned to Britain.

It is in the holds that the ship begins to come alive. The cargo was packed tight – 5,000 bales of wool could be carried – and little thought was given to the comfort of the crew. Originally their quarters were tucked tight into the bows, although later they were moved to the relative comfort of the deck. The officers by contrast, had quite comfortable accommodation, with even a coal fire. Imagine being a ship's boy some time in the late 19th century (no less than 30 were taken on the *Cutty Sark*), scrambling up the rigging as the ship bucked and heaved through the waves and water swirled over the deck.

Royal Naval College The entrance to the Royal Naval College – which is still in use as a training establishment for naval officers – is just behind *Cutty Sark*. Only two buildings are open to the public, the Chapel and the Painted Hall. It was beneath the sumptuously decorated ceiling of the Painted Hall that Nelson lay in state after he was killed at the Battle of Trafalgar in 1805, and crowds flocked to pay tribute to the national hero. The ceiling shows William and Mary, the Dutch monarchs who took over the English throne in 1688, handing the cup of liberty to Europe, amid a lot of very ornate detail.

National Maritime Museum The National Maritime Museum occupies the Queen's House (currently closed for extensive repairs) and two wings which were built later and linked by an elegant colonnade. The most interesting displays are in the west wing, which is where your visit should begin. A good starting-point would be New Neptune Hall. Here you can board the paddle tug *Reliant.* Almost the entire ship has been preserved. You can see the master's cabin, the crew's quarters and the stoke-hold where the boilers were fired. *Reliant,* launched in 1907 and in service until 1969, was the last working vessel powered by side-lever engines, which are still in full working order. Large Navy vessels and liners had already started to go over from paddles to screw propellers as early as the 1860s.

In the next-door hall are displayed the royal barges, all magnificently decorated. As well as the royal family, senior Admiralty officials used them to visit the Royal Dockyards at Deptford (see walk 11) and at Woolwich.

Another part of the museum of especial interest is the section on marine archaeology, where replicas of the Ferriby boats, found on the shore of the river Humber, are shown. These are the oldest boats found anywhere outside Egypt. Also worth seeing is *The Way of a Ship,* which consists of six fascinating slide presentations explaining in detail how a large sailing vessel works.

These are just a few highlights from the Museum. It is well worth spending as much time here as you can.

Greenwich Town   In the town there are plenty of interesting shops and good places to eat. MacDonalds Restaurant on King William Walk (*not* part of the well-known fast food chain) serves reasonable food at reasonable prices. There is an antiques market on Saturday and Sunday mornings on the corner of the High Street and Croom's Hill where you can buy china, glass, etc. and a good selection of knick-knacks, records, books, clothes and so on. Collectors of 1950s items would do well here; prices are moderate. The lovely covered market between College Approach and Nelson Road has craft stalls at weekends.

Tunnel to the Isle of Dogs   An interesting short excursion leads under the Thames to the Isle of Dogs. The tunnel entrance is via the curious dome on the riverfront, just to the left of the ferry pier as you face the water. Its partner is visible across the river. A handsome old-fashioned lift takes you down to the passageway itself, or you can gallop down the stairs. The tunnel, stretching out into the distance, would make an excellent roller-skating run – but doubtless that's not allowed. The best thing about the north bank is the stunning view back across to Greenwich. Walk here for a while, as the view alters perspective as you move.

The two main walks from Greenwich are east along the river, towards the Blackwall Tunnel, and round Greenwich Park, taking in the Royal Observatory.

River Walk The river walk runs in front of the Naval College, past the Trafalgar Tavern, which in the 19th century used to serve an annual dinner of whitebait to the Cabinet, whose members travelled down by barge from Westminster for the occasion. Then you pass a lovely early 17th-century building which is Trinity Hospital. It was founded in 1613 and has served as a home for elderly men ever since. Immediately behind it is Greenwich Power Station, which nowadays is owned by London Regional Transport. It provides supplementary power for the London Underground network at busy times when the main LRT power supply from Lots Road would otherwise be overloaded. At Ballast Quay a house is still named the Harbour Master's Office, though it no longer serves as such. In the late 18th century, Execution Dock, where pirates were hanged, was moved here from Wapping (see walk 11). From here on the walk runs past a fascinating mixture of factories and quays, and you realize that the Thames is still a working river. The path stops near the Blackwall Tunnel after about 3 kilometres (2 miles), and although you can return along roads, the same route back is much nicer, with a number of excellent and unexpected views of the Naval College.

Park Walk Greenwich Park is one of London's most perfect places – and that despite the fact that its landscape is all a bad mistake. The park had already been a royal park for well over 200 years before Charles II commissioned the French landscape artist Le Nôtre to redesign it in the then fashionable French style. Le Nôtre fulfilled his commission – but without ever visiting London and, crucially, without ever appreciating that a long ridge divides the park into two. As a result the formal entrance road from Blackheath simply stops short when it reaches the edge of the hill, which drops sharply down towards the Queen's House.

The best parts of the park are the Flower Garden on the south-east side and, behind it, The Wilderness. Deer were introduced to the park in 1515, and the lovely creatures you see here are the descendants of those first arrivals. Henry VIII and Anne Boleyn danced round Queen Elizabeth's Oak on the east side of the park. There is irony in that, for on May Day 1536 Anne dropped her handkerchief at a tournament as a signal to her lover. Henry noticed and within 24 hours Anne, her brother and their associates had been carted off to the Tower. The Ranger's House on the west edge of the park is a lovely late 17th-century house where there is now a splendid collection of portraits.

There is a pleasant Tea House in the middle of the park, near the central ride from Blackheath.

Old Royal Observatory (Flamsteed House) You must of course leave time for the Old Royal Observatory, for here, in a manner of speaking, is the source of time itself. In the late 17th century, when urban pollution was unheard of, Charles II established the Royal Observatory here, and for nearly 300 years much pioneering astronomical work was done under the direction of a series of distinguished Astronomers Royal, the title given to the director of the Royal Observatory. After the Second World War, London's grime became too much, and the Royal Observatory moved to Herstmonceux in Sussex.

The Greenwich Meridian and Greenwich Mean Time are world famous. The Meridian is the 0° longitude line, on which navigators everywhere base their calculations. Greenwich Mean Time is the world zero for time. Until railways were built, more or less every town worked on its own time. In Britain, London was a few minutes ahead of Reading, which was a few minutes ahead of Bristol. That didn't matter much when hardly anyone travelled far, and if they did it was very slowly. But once trains started to run, and timetables began to be written, chaos resulted. People used to arrive at a junction expecting to change into a connecting train, only to find that it was running on a different time and had already left. By the 1840s Greenwich time – nicknamed 'railway time' – was being used everywhere in Britain, and 40 years later it became standard throughout the world. The different time zones across the globe are still described as so many hours behind or in front of Greenwich Mean Time.

The red ball – known as the Greenwich time ball – on the roof of the Observatory (now called Flamsteed House) was the first visual time signal in the world when it was put up in 1833. It continues to drop every day at precisely 1.00pm as a signal to river traffic, having been hauled up its pole a few minutes earlier. The 24-hour clock set in the gatepost of Flamsteed House operates the ball; it always shows Greenwich Mean Time, even in the summer when our clocks are one hour ahead on British Summer Time.

Inside Flamsteed House there is a fascinating and quite complex series of displays on astronomical topics. The Octagon Room where Flamsteed – the first and one of the greatest Astronomers Royal – made his observations has been furnished much as it was in his day. The Meridian Building contains telescopes and other instruments, and a fascinating exhibition on time and its measurement, with all manner of equipment, from astrolabes to atomic clocks, on display. And, of course, you can stand with feet straddling the Meridian, a foot in each hemisphere, east and west. Demonstrations and lectures are frequently given in the Planetarium.

Gipsy Moth IV

c/o CS Cutty Sark
King William Walk
Greenwich
London SE10
Tel: 01-858 3445
Opening times: summer: Mondays to Saturdays 10.30am-6.00pm, Sundays 12.00-6.00pm; closed in winter

CS Cutty Sark
King William Walk
Greenwich
London SE10
Tel: 01-858 3445
Opening times: summer: Mondays to Saturdays
10.30 am-6.00 pm, Sundays 12.00-6.00 pm; winter:
Mondays to Saturdays 10.30 am-5.00 pm, Sundays
12.00-5.00 pm

Royal Naval College
Greenwich
London SE10
Tel: 01-858 2154
Opening times: daily except Thursdays 2.30-5.00 pm
Admission only to the Painted Hall and the Chapel; the
College may be closed to the public at short notice

National Maritime Museum
Greenwich
London SE10 9NF
Tel: 01-858 4422
Opening times: summer: Mondays to Saturdays
10.00 am-.00 pm, Sundays 2.00-5.30 pm; winter:
Mondays to Fridays 10.00 am-5.00 pm, Saturdays
10.00 am-5.30 pm, Sundays 2.00-5.00 pm; closed
some Bank Holidays

Ranger's House
Chesterfield Walk
Blackheath
London SE10
Tel: 01-853 0035
Opening times: February to October: daily
10.00 am-5.00 pm; November to January: daily
10.00 am-4.00 pm

Old Royal Observatory

Greenwich Park
Greenwich
London SE10
Tel: 01-858 4422
Opening times: summer: Mondays to Saturdays
10.00am-6.00pm, Sundays 2.00-5.00pm; winter:
Mondays to Fridays 10.00am-5.00pm, Saturdays
10.00-5.30pm, Sundays 2.00-5.00pm; closed some
Bank Holidays

13   HAMPSTEAD AND HIGHGATE

Start: Belsize Park Underground Station
Bus: 268

Finish: Archway Underground Station
Buses: 19, 27, 41, 45, 137, 143, 153, 263

Distance: 9·6 kilometres (6 miles)

Places to sit down: Hampstead Heath
                           Waterlow Park

Eating places: The Buttery, Burgh House
                     Louis's Patisserie, Fitzjohn's Avenue
                     Kenwood House, Hampstead Heath

City, village and countryside are normally quite distant from each other. In Hampstead and Highgate, high on the northern hills that overlook central London, you will find all three in close proximity. Both Hampstead and Highgate have all the attributes of a big city: a cosmopolitan population and sophisticated shops and restaurants. Yet life here is lived in a setting as perfect as that of any country village. And then, seemingly everywhere in this area, there is Hampstead Heath: 320 hectares (800 acres) of green, much of it remarkably deserted and wild, where even on a sunny summer's day it is easy to escape the crowds.

This excursion is for those who want to enjoy a breathing space away from the pavements of central London and to relax in the fresher air of the hills. Allow at least an afternoon, or better still an entire day, especially if you want a good walk on the Heath. The route described is simply a suggestion. The best way to enjoy both villages and Heath is to meander where the fancy takes you.

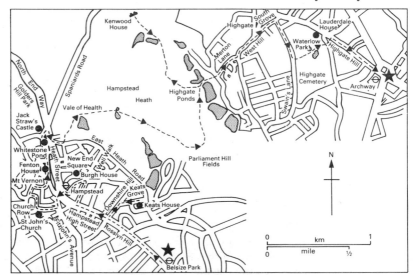

Downshire Hill From Belsize Park Underground Station turn north up Rosslyn Hill and then right after about ½ mile down Downshire Hill. Like many other streets in Hampstead, Downshire Hill possesses a simple elegance and balance, with attractive early 19th-century houses and a chapel on the corner of Keats Grove.

Keats House About halfway down Keats Grove you turn into the garden of Keats House and immediately expect to meet the poet himself. Little seems to have changed since John Keats came to live here in 1818. There is still a plum tree in the garden, the successor to the one under which 'Ode to a Nightingale' was written, and inside the house is furnished much as it was in those years. Letters, manuscripts and other Keats memorabilia are on display, including a lock of Fanny Brawne's hair. Fanny, whose family shared the house with Keats, became engaged to the poet in 1819. They never married, for Keats died two years later in Rome.

Well Walk From Keats House you can either make for the Heath, one long finger of which extends to the far end of Keats Grove, or return along Downshire Hill and turn right along the High Street towards the centre of the village. Turn right again along Gayton Road. This leads into Well Walk, which commemorates the spa waters that first drew people of fashion to Hampstead. A pump room was built here in 1701, and for a few decades the chalybeate waters (that is, containing iron) of Hampstead were all the rage. Visitors flocked to the Assembly Room to dance and hear the latest gossip and to the Pump Room to take the waters. Of these, and of a later building known as the Long Room, nothing now remains, although a Victorian fountain does stand where the spring once flowed. Take care, though: the water is no longer fit to drink.

Burgh House Just off Well Walk you come to New End Square and Burgh House, a lovely 18th-century house that now, after a chequered career which almost came to a conclusion with demolition 20 years ago, belongs to a voluntary trust, the Burgh House Trust. In the basement there is a pleasant and fairly cheap café (one of the few reasonably priced eating establishments in Hampstead) known as the Buttery, where a notice requests you, in the politest terms possible, to be 'so helpful' and clear away your dirty crockery. The floors above are used as a community centre, with frequent exhibitions and social activities.

The attractive streets around New End Square are well worth strolling through. Flask Walk leads back to the High Street, past The Old Wells and Campden Baths Wash Houses, dating from 1888 but now converted into a private house. Gone are the days when houses in Hampstead lacked bathrooms.

Hampstead Village The centre of Hampstead village is at the junction of the High Street and Heath Street, which climbs steeply uphill to Whitestone Pond (see below). Hampstead Underground Station on the corner is the deepest in the London system, with platforms which are 59 metres (194 feet) below street level. The original lifts installed when the station was opened in 1907 are now on show in the London Transport Museum (see walk 4). The building opposite was for a long time the local fire station, look-out being kept from the watch tower.

Turn down Fitzjohn's Avenue, past Louis's Patisserie, which sells good things but is almost always packed with people. The alleyways running between the High Street and Fitzjohn's Avenue have interesting shops and are worth exploring.

Church Row Now turn right into Church Row. This lovely little street of early 18th-century houses must find a place on almost any list of London's top ten perfect places. If you can mentally remove the rows of parked cars – they are everywhere in Hampstead and all too often spoil the intimacy of the streets – it hardly seems as if anything has changed for 250 years. Even most of the railings are original.

St John's Church at the end of Church Row draws the street to a beautifully balanced conclusion. The Suffolk painter John Constable and his wife are buried in the churchyard. Although he is best known for his paintings of East Anglia, Constable spent the last 18 years of his life, from 1819 to 1837, in various houses in Hampstead, and did some fine paintings of the Heath. These can be seen in the Tate Gallery and the Victoria and Albert Museum.

Mount Vernon Turn right along Frognal and then right at the end into Mount Vernon again. You could almost be in a Mediterranean village here, with secluded cottages clinging to the hillside amidst a profusion of flowers. The Vernon of Mount Vernon was a General Charles Vernon, who was Governor of the Tower of London and apparently had 'the worst temper of any man alive'.

Fenton House Bear right up Hampstead Grove, past the entrance to Fenton House, thought to be the oldest surviving house in Hampstead and now owned by the National Trust. It is a friendly looking place, built in 1693 and bought a century later by a merchant named Philip Fenton, from whom it takes its name. The drawingroom on the first floor is furnished as it was in the early 19th century and shows how wealthy, though not aristocratic, people lived. The house contains two major collections: of early musical instruments and of porcelain and pottery.

Whitestone Pond Continue the gentle climb up Hampstead Grove, which soon comes out at Whitestone Pond. This is a favourite haunt of everyone, young and old alike, who enjoys sailing model boats. The views over central London on a fine day are fabulous, as they are everywhere along the ridge here. The pond is so called from the milestone almost at the top of Heath Street, which tells us that we are 4½ miles and 29 yards from Holborn Bars. The pub just beyond is Jack Straw's Castle. Jack Straw was one of the leaders of the Peasant's Revolt in 1381, and was responsible for burning down a priory in Clerkenwell, near the present site of Smithfield Market. He hid here after the collapse of the rebellion, but was eventually captured and executed.

Golders Hill Park Off North End, the main road that leads downhill away from Hampstead towards Golders Green, lies Golders Hill Park. This extension of the Heath is a pleasant place to walk and has a small zoo and a tea house.

The route back into Hampstead Village is straight down Heath Street, which is full of expensive restaurants and the exhaust fumes of cars grinding slowly up the hill. The Milk Churn on the left has good ice-creams to take away, but if you sit down inside to eat a sundae it will cost you rather more. A more pleasant alternative route is down East Heath Road, then right through the network of lovely streets and so back to the High Street.

Vale of Health A road running left of East Heath Road takes you down to the curiously named Vale of Health. Until the late 18th century this was a vale of ill-health, an uninhabited area of swampy marshland infected with malaria. When it was drained it was rechristened, presumably in an attempt to attract residents to the houses that were built here.

Hampstead Heath And so, at long last, to the wide open spaces of the Heath. It is a matter of very good fortune, and the happy result of an early conservation battle, that the Heath is still here at all. Until well into the 19th century the land was open countryside, common land on which people from the village (for Hampstead was a true country village then, with open fields between it and London) had for centuries held the right to graze their cattle. The Lord of the Manor of Hampstead, one Sir Spencer Maryon Wilson, who lived on the far side of London at Charlton, near Greenwich, had other ideas. He realized that London was expanding fast, and decided to cash in on the expansion. In 1829 he claimed the right, under a 13th-century law, to enclose the common land, extract sand and gravel from it, and then build houses on it. An influential committee – Hampstead then was full of influential people, as it still is – was formed to oppose him: successfully, as it turned out in the end, but not before some 40 years of arguments and protests and meetings had passed and not until Sir Spencer himself had died. The Metropolitan Board of Works (the 19th-century predecessor of the GLC) acquired the first 100 hectares (240 acres) in the 1870s, and Parliament Hill Fields, Golders Hill and the house and grounds at Kenwood were added over the next half century.

Parliament Hill Parliament Hill, on the south-east side of the Heath, is the most open part, and the top of the hill is a favourite place for kite-flying. Why the Parliament in the title? No one knows for certain. Some historians believe that a Saxon Folk-Moot (a very early version of Parliament) may have met on top of the hill. Others claim that Guy Fawkes and his associates (see walk 2) planned to watch Parliament burning from here.

The landscape in the northerly parts of the Heath is more

varied, with patches of gorse and shrub mixed in with woodland sections. The amount of woodland is gradually increasing, and the Heath is much less heathlike than it was 200 years ago. You can still find deserted spots where you can laze all day and hardly see another person. The northern extension of the Heath, on the north side of Spaniards Road, the link road across the ridge to Highgate, is also relatively unvisited.

Kenwood House Kenwood House, at the north-east side of the heath just south of Hampstead Lane, is one of the most pleasant and friendly aristocratic homes open to the public in London. The first mansion on the site was built in 1616. It was almost completely rebuilt at the end of the 17th century and then, not much more than 50 years later, it was the subject of another improvement and remodelling scheme undertaken by Robert Adam. Humphrey Repton, the foremost landscape designer of his day, was brought in 25 years later to create the gardens. Inside, the library is the masterpiece – but each of the rooms is lovely, a fitting setting for the Iveagh Bequest, a magnificent collection of paintings including works by Rembrandt, Vermeer, Gainsborough, Landseer, Reynolds and many others. There are two refreshment places: a restaurant in what used to be the kitchens, and a pleasant snack bar in the former brewery.

The grounds are pleasant to wander round, and there are plenty of seats. Spring brings a spectacular display of rhododendrons and azaleas. If the weather holds, and not too many planes pass overhead, the summer Saturday evening concerts are wonderful occasions. You sit on deckchairs or – much more fun, and cheaper too – on the grass, with the orchestra playing on the far side of the lake and the music wafting across the water.

Highgate Village Highgate Village, on the far side of the Heath from Hampstead, makes a good finale to a walk round the Heath. From Highgate Ponds above Parliament Hill take Merton Lane and then West Hill up towards the centre of the village. Highgate has always been crowded with travellers. For centuries it was the first stopping-place on the way north out of London, and refreshment was available at the many inns for travellers and, rather more important in view of the steepness of the hill just climbed, for their horses.

135

Highgate Cemetery One of Highgate's most famous landmarks is the cemetery – or, to be accurate, the two cemeteries – reached by turning down Swain's Lane from South Grove, which leads off West Hill. The East Cemetery is still in use, and is only worth a look for the grave of Karl Marx, which is surmounted by a large bust. His famous slogans 'Workers of the world unite' and 'Philosophers have only interpreted the world. The point, however, is to change it' are inscribed around the base of the plinth. Marx settled in London in 1849 and died there in 1883, having written many of his works in the reading room of the British Museum. The grave is usually surrounded by large groups of official tourists from eastern Europe, the USSR or China.

The original, western, cemetery is quite different: a crazed Hollywood film set, it would seem at first glance, the product of someone's over-vivid imagination (indeed, a number of horror movies have been made here). It's a far cry from the respectable Victorian resting-place for respectable Victorian citizens that the London Cemetery Company set out to provide when it opened the gates here in 1839. Highgate soon became the fashionable place to be buried. If you – or, rather, your body – had been brought here in 1900, say, you would have joined the august company of the poet Christina Rossetti; Michael Faraday, famous for his work on electricity; Carl Rosa, founder of the celebrated opera company; and many more. Your grieving family might have had an elaborate tomb or monument designed, perhaps decorated with stone angels and embellished with a fulsomely worded tribute to your life and works.

What then has come to pass, and why is the cemetery in such a state? The simple answer is lack of money. The United Cemetery Company (the successor to the founding London Cemetery Company) has long been short of cash, and could not undertake the considerable amount of day-to-day maintenance necessary; for many years little or no work was done at all. The cemetery became increasingly overgrown, a wildlife sanctuary scarcely visited by humans, except for the vandals who broke in from time to time. In the end, after a period in which it seemed that the cemetery might be sold, the western part was acquired by the Friends of Highgate Cemetery; the eastern part is run by the local council.

The Friends now operate several tours a day round the cemetery, as well as undertaking a limited amount of restoration and maintenance work. On four days a year you can wander round unguided, and if you can manage to come on one of these days, do so. The tour, although interesting, can be rather long-drawn-out, although you are shown the amazing catacombs and many interesting graves which you might otherwise miss. If you have a taste for the slightly macabre and exotic, you will enjoy yourself here. But don't come if you are at all likely to be upset.

Waterlow Park On the opposite side of Swain's Lane is the entrance to Waterlow Park, given by Sir Sidney Waterlow to the local community in 1889 as 'a garden for those who are gardenless'. The story is told that, when Sir Sidney visited the park for the last time four years later, all the children playing there were brought together to cheer their benefactor. The park has three ponds, each at a different level of the hillside, with lots of wild life. It's an extremely pleasant place to stop and relax.

Lauderdale House At the top of the park you come to Lauderdale House. Originally built in the 16th century, and remodelled in the 1640s, the house was borrowed from its owner, the Earl of Lauderdale, by Charles II, who installed his mistress Nell Gwynne there. It is said that Nell, annoyed because the king had refused to give a title to their son, threatened to drop the young child out of a window. A bit of quick thinking on Charles' part saved the day, and he called out 'Save the Earl of Burford'. But that story is told of other houses too, and so one can wonder whether it really did happen. The house was badly damaged by fire in the 1960s and is now used as a local arts and community centre.

Highgate Hill On the opposite side of Highgate Hill stands Cromwell House, built in the 1630s. The name Cromwell was only bestowed on it in the 19th century, and there is no known connection with Oliver Cromwell, the Lord Protector of England. Nor, it seems, is the famous story about what happened to the philosopher Francis Bacon on Highgate

Hill true. Legend has it that as he was travelling up the hill one day in 1626 he was thinking about the problem of how to keep food fresh. Seeing a chicken scuttling about, he got out of his coach, had the bird killed and then stuffed it with snow to see how fast it would decay. Bacon might now be known as the inventor of deep-freezing. But unfortunately his experiment did for him as well as for the chicken; he caught a chill and died soon after.

Whittington Stone The final leg of the route is down Highgate Hill, past the Whittington Stone that is said to mark the spot where Dick Whittington heard the chimes of Bow Bells calling him back to London. Sad to relate, the story is probably pure myth. There was indeed a real Dick Whittington, who was Lord Mayor four times and who, dying childless, left all his money to charity. But there is no evidence that he ever left London to seek his fortune, nor any that he possessed a cat.

The walk finishes at the foot of Highgate Hill, by Archway Underground Station.

Keats House

Wentworth Place
Keats Grove
London NW3 2RR
Tel: 01-435 2062
Opening times: daily 10.00am-1.00pm,
2.00-6.00pm; closed some Bank Holidays

Fenton House

Hampstead Grove
London NW3
Tel: 01-435 3471
Opening times: March: Saturdays and Sundays
only 11.00am-6.00pm; April to October: daily except
Thursdays and Fridays 11.00am-6.00pm; last
admission 1 hour before closing time

The Iveagh Bequest
Kenwood
Hampstead Lane
London NW3 7JR
Tel: 01-348 1286
Opening times: April to September: daily
10.00am-7.00pm; February, March and October:
daily 10.00am-5.00pm; November to January: daily
10.00am-4.00pm

Highgate Cemetery
Swain's Lane
London N6 6PJ
Tel: 01-340 1834
Guided tours daily on the hour April to September:
10.00am-4.00pm; October to March:
10.00am-3.00pm; four special open days a year

EATING OUT

Many restaurateurs are happy to admit children, as long as they are accompanied by adults. With the exception of fast-food restaurants and cafés, it is always advisable to ring first and check because some restaurateurs have a policy of admitting, say, over-fives or over tens only; others welcome children only at lunch-times or in the early evening.

It is sensible to book a table in all but the fast-food restaurants, cafés and coffee shops and to order children's portions in advance. Restaurateurs who do not advertise a separate children's menu or children's portions may well be willing to prepare a favourite dish or something not listed on the standard menu if they are given time to plan for it.

When booking, check opening times, prices and other details listed below. The information given was correct at the time of going to press, but restaurateurs change their menus, restructure their opening hours, upgrade their price lists and close for refurbishment at regular intervals.

All chefs and waiting staff have off days, but their customers – children included – are entitled to good food and polite service. If you are dissatisfied, make a complaint to the waiter or waitress; if he or she fails to deal with the problem, a quiet word with the manager will usually elicit results. Complain immediately; the manager is there to keep the clientele happy, but can do little about a complaint made by a customer on the point of leaving.

Barnes **Old Rangoon**

201 Castelnau
London, SW13
Tel: 741 9656
Buses: 9, 33, 72
Underground: Hammersmith
Open: noon-11.30 pm every day
Average prices: starters 95p-£3.15; salads £3.25-£3.95; mains £3.50-£4.25; puddings £1.75-£1.95; beverages 50p-70p; children half price.
Credit cards: Access; AmEx; Diners Club; Visa
This former pub is a super place to take children, who are charged half price for the international 'British Empire' dishes (satay, potato skins with chilli and sour cream, poppadoms, chicken tikka and teriyaki and barbecued ribs, steaks and hamburger*) and £1 for a set children's tea, consisting of soft drinks, sandwiches, chocolate biscuits and the like. You can eat on the terrace or take one of their picnic hampers into the huge walled and landscaped garden (they provide a blanket to sit on), where there are ducks, rabbits and doves, a children's play area, a waterfall, and floodlighting in the evenings.
*one only on menu

Camden Town **Marine Ices**

8 Haverstock Hill
London, NW3
Tel: 485 8898
Buses: 31, 68
Underground: Chalk Farm
Open: 10.30 am-10.45 pm Mon-Sat; 11 am-6 pm Sun (ice creams, patisserie and beverages only)
Average prices: minimum charge £2.50 a head; noon-3 pm, 6-10.45 pm Mon-Sat; antipasti 80p-£2; pizzas and pasta £1-£2.60; veal and chicken £3.75-£4.20; ice creams 45p-£1; beverages 30p-60p.

140

Credit cards: Luncheon Vouchers only
The marvellous Italian ice creams, sorbets, cassate, bombes and sundaes
made on the premises are a perennial favourite with children, so this is a
great place to end a visit to Camden Lock. The street-level restaurant is
large enough to accommodate the odd push chair, with plenty of space
between tables. For lunch or dinner there's a short menu of deliciously
fresh antipasti, pasta, veal, chicken and hot, crisp pizzas. Babies are
welcome and children's portions available.

One-Legged Goose

17 Princess Road
London, NW1
Tel: 722 9665
Bus: 74
Underground: Camden Town, Chalk Farm
Open: noon-2.30pm Mon-Fri, Sun (lunch); 7pm-11.15pm Mon-Sat
7pm-10.30pm Sun (dinner)
Average prices: Starters £1.95-£2.95; mains £4.95-£6.95; desserts
£1.95.
Credit cards: AmEx; Visa.
This restaurant is warmly inviting in winter and has a covered garden with
a barbecue that is very popular in summer. The menu is an interesting
international mixture – Italian pasta dishes, rack of lamb, Cumbrian
hotpot, potato skins – and appealing to children. Sunday lunch, at £3.25
for children, is the attraction for parents here.

Chelsea ## Huffs

Chelsea Farmer's Market
250 King's Road (entrance on Sydney Street)
London, SW3
Tel: 352 5600
Buses: 11, 19, 22, 49
Open: 10am-6pm every day
Average prices: Snacks from 95p; main dishes from £2.95; patisserie
about £1; beverages 40p-75p. Unlicensed.
The Chelsea Farmer's Market is a complex of shops (a butcher, a cheese
shop, a fish shop with a small trout farm, a wholefood shop, a fruit and veg
stall, a pet supplies shop and a garden centre) in a large fenced-off area
just off the King's Road, opposite The Reject Shop. Just inside the
entrance is Huffs, a counter-service café in a conservatory. The
wholesome salads, pies, cakes and sandwiches arrayed along the counter
are almost irresistible. This is a pleasant respite from a Saturday shopping
session on the crowded King's Road. Park prams and pushchairs outside
in winter (there are steps up to the café) or eat at one of the outdoor tables
and let children play around on the paths and (artificial) grass.

City ## The Fish Inn

110 Old Street
London, EC1
Tel: 251 3937
Buses: 5, 55, 243

Underground: Barbican, Old Street
Open: 11.30am-10.30pm Mon-Fri.
Prices: starters 80p-£1.80; fish £2 (mackerel) – £5.35 (large Dover sole); pizzas £1.95 (small) – £4.90 (large); other mains £1.50-£3; desserts 65p-£1.50; beverages 25p-£1; children's menu £1.
Credit cards: Access; AmEx.
City restaurants are rarely called upon to serve children, this City fish and chippie being one of the few exceptions. The takeaway is in the front and the restaurant, at the back and downstairs, is decorated with instructive posters illustrating fish and shellfish species and photographs of early 20th-century London. The fish, with the thinnest possible coating of batter, is cooked to an appetising golden brown and the chips are perfectly crisp. They also serve 16 different pizzas, burgers, chicken and Cornish pasties and other pies. You can have soft drinks, good tea or cappuccino, milk shakes, wines (some by the half bottle) and even cocktails and spirits with your meal. The Fish Inn is unique among fish and chip restaurants in offering a 'Kiddie's Corner' menu; £1 for a small cod and chips, dessert and coke.

Covent Garden
Bates
11 Henrietta Street
London, WC2
Tel: 240 7600
Buses: 1, 1A, 9, 11, 13, 15, 23, 24, 29, 77, 77A, 170, 176
Underground: Covent Garden, Leicester Square
Open: noon-3pm Mon-Fri, Sun (lunch); 5.30-11.30pm Mon-Sat, 5.30-10.30pm Sun (dinner)
Average prices: starters £2; mains £5.30; all puddings £1.90; coffee with mints 65p; set roast lunch on Sundays £4.90 (two courses), £6.85 (including pudding). Children half price.
Credit cards: Access; AmEx; Diners Club; Keith Prowse; Visa.
An elegant, palm-decorated restaurant with comfortable seating, serving adventurous British food. The quiet, efficient staff welcome both babies and children, who may colour the paper tablecloths with the crayons provided while you finish your coffee. Bates' set Sunday lunch is excellent value and a popular family occasion in the Garden.

Calabash
38 King Street
London, WC2
Tel: 836 1976
Buses: 1, 1A, 9, 11, 13, 15, 23, 24, 29, 77, 77A, 170, 176
Underground: Covent Garden
Open: noon-3pm Mon-Fri (lunch); 6-11pm Mon-Sat (dinner)
Average prices: starters £1.50-£1.70; mains £2.90-£3.75; veg 70p-£1.40; puddings 90p-£1.60.
Credit cards: AmEx; Diners Club; Visa.
A delightful restaurant, hidden in the basement of the Africa Centre and decorated with a variety of African artefacts. The menu changes regularly to encompass dishes from all over Africa. Babies are not admitted, but small portions are available for older children, who may enjoy some of the

simpler dishes, such as the Senegalese fried fish in tomato sauce served
with rice, the West African chicken in peanut butter sauce or the
Zanzibari chicken cooked in coconut cream. An unusual and quiet haven
in the Garden with a relaxed atmosphere and pleasant – if sometimes
slow – service; the staff take pains to explain the menu.

Diana's Diner

39 Endell Street
London, WC2
Tel: 240 0272
Buses: 19, 22, 25, 38, 55
Underground: Covent Garden
Open: 9am-2pm Mon-Fri; 9am-2pm Sat
Average prices: minimum charge noon-3pm £1.50 (no sandwiches);
snacks and sandwiches 60p-£1.50; salads £1-£2.50; mains £1.60-£4.50;
beverages 45p-80p.
Credit cards: Luncheon vouchers only.
A small, cheerful café with the friendliest service and possibly the
cheapest prices in the Garden. They willingly serve children's portions of
sausage, egg, beans, burgers and the like with chips or on toast and their
menu includes milk shakes, soft drinks and fresh orange juice. Eat at their
pavement tables in summer. Famed in the area for pleasant service.

Porters

17 Henrietta Street
London, WC2
Tel: 836 6466
Buses: 1, 1A, 9, 11, 13, 15, 23, 24, 29, 77, 77A, 170, 176
Underground: Covent Garden
Open: noon-3pm daily (lunch); 5.30-11.30pm Mon-Sat; 5.30-10.30pm
Sun (dinner).
Average prices: pies £2.70-£3.40 and veg 60p-85p; puddings £1-£1.15;
coffee/soft drinks 45p; set roast lunch £3.85 (adults), £2.30 (children) at
weekends only.
Credit cards: Access; Visa.
A traditional English pie-and-pudding restaurant in an old fruit and veg
warehouse. Their cottage, chicken and leek and fish pies are all cheap,
good and large and puddings include steamed syrup sponge, treacle tart
and bread and butter pudding. Service is relaxed and children welcome.
There's plenty of space, seating for 250 and high chairs for babies.

Holland Park

Mario's in Holland Park

Holland Park (between the Orangery and Holland House)
London, W8
Tel: 602 2216 (bookings not accepted)
Buses: 9, 12, 28, 31, 73, 88
Underground: Holland Park
Open: 10.30am-8pm (summer), closes at dusk in winter.
Average price: sandwiches and patisserie about £1; salads £2.50.
A pleasant, self-service café, run by an Italian family, in the centre of
Holland Park. They serve good, fresh soup, sandwiches, cakes and salads,
as well as tea, coffee, milk and soft drinks. Eat inside in winter (it's warm

and there's room for baby buggies) and at tables outside in the walled garden in summer.

Holborn
My Old Dutch
131 High Holborn
London, WC1
Tel: 242 5200
Buses: 8, 19, 22, 38
Underground: Holborn
Open: noon-11.30pm Mon-Thur, Sun; 12.30-11.130pm Fri, Sat.
Average prices: pancakes £1.85-£3.05; waffles 95p-£1.25; desserts 75p-£2.65; beverages 35p-75p.
Credit cards: Access; AmEx; Diners Club; Luncheon Vouchers; Visa.
Children adore novelties and will be amazed at the 18″ diameter of the pancakes in My Old Dutch (small children had better share one). There are a staggering 67 different fillings to choose from. Bookings are not accepted here but the large, two-floor restaurant tends to be full only on Friday and Saturday evenings. A fun place for a treat.

Knightsbridge
Harrods New England Ice Cream Parlour
Knightsbridge
London, SW1
Tel: 730 1234
Buses: 9, 14, 52, 73, 74
Underground: Knightsbridge
Open: 9am-4.45pm Mon, Tue, Thurs, Fri; 9.30am-6.45pm Wed; 9am-5.45pm Sat
Average prices: Ice creams 80p-£2.35
If you are shopping in Knightsbridge, the Ice Cream Parlour on the ground floor of Harrods (enter from Hans Crescent or Basil Street on Knightsbridge tube side) is a convenient place to take children. The parlour is, in fact, a counter with bar stools serving ice creams and sundaes, frozen yoghurts and very good coffee. Prices are a little above average because New England ice creams are made from pure fresh cream. The parlour becomes very crowded afer 11am but service is instant and the turn-around fast.

Leicester Square/
Trafalgar Square
area
Café Pelican
45 St Martin's Land (Trafalgar Square end)
London, WC2
Tel: 379 0309
Buses: 1, 24, 29, 176
Underground: Leicester Square
Open: 11am-2am every day.
Average prices: £1.50-6.25 (café); menu promotionnel (three courses plus coffee, nouvelle cuisine-sized portions) £10.95; starters £2.95-£3.95; mains £6.90-£11.45; desserts £1.50-£3.50; beverages 65p-£1.50. Children half price.
Credit cards: Account customers; Access; AmEx; Diners Club; Visa.
The Café Pélican is an elegant French brasserie – a café-restaurant – where you can have breakfast, a snack, lunch, tea or dinner. It was

designed with family patronage in mind; there are baby-changing facilities in the loos, high chairs and half-price children's portions, toilets for the elderly and access for wheelchairs. Restaurant meals are expensive – about £30 for two – although not overpriced considering the deservedly high reputation of the chef, Gerard Mosiniak. In the café at the front, however, you can order just a coffee, sandwiches (£1.50) or a or a croque monsieur (a toasted ham and cheese sandwich) with salad (£3.95), their marvellous French onion soup (£2.95) or plate of French cheeses (£3.25), all served with delicious French bread, plus coffee. Best of all, go for tea. The Chef Patissier trained under Mosimann at the Dorchester and his pastries are superlative. Service is usually charming, but at busy times you'll experience the kind of service the French call brisk and the English, brusque.

Lyons Corner House

450 Strand (Trafalgar Square end)
London, WC2
Tel: 930 9281
Open: 8am-8pm every day
Buses: 1, 1A, 6, 9, 11, 13, 15, 23, 77, 77A, 170, 172, 176
BR Station/Underground: Charing Cross.
Average prices: minimum charge noon-7pm £1.75; starters 40p-£1.45; mains £1.70-£4.35; puddings 45p-£1.35; set meals £2.65 (breakfasts, 8am-noon); £4.45 (three courses, from noon); £1.95 (teas, 3-5.30pm). Children's menu; £1.75 (main course, pudding and a drink).
Credit cards: Access; AmEx; Diners Club; Luncheon Vouchers, Visa.
The new look Lyons is a bright and airy restaurant, large enough to be rarely overcrowded, even on Saturdays. Upstairs is a coffee shop, serving breakfasts, burgers, salads and snacks and afternoon teas, and there's a restaurant downstairs. Like the original Lyons, this is a family restaurant; they have high chairs and booster seats for babies and toddlers and Heinz baby foods. Ask one of the uniformed 'nippies' (younger and cooler than their motherly predecessors, but attentive), for their 'Children's Choice' menu for under 12s. Lyons also cater for children's parties, contact the Manager for details.

Peppermint Park

13-14 Upper St Martin's Lane
London, WC2
Tel: 836 5234
Buses: 1, 24, 29, 176
Underground: Leicester Square
Open: 12.30pm-1.30am every day
Average prices: snacks/starters: £1.50-£3.25; mains: £1.95-£5; side orders 30p-90p; beverages 60p-80p; kiddyburger with chips (for under 13s) £1.95 Mon-Sat; free Sun.
Credit cards: Access; AmEx; Diners Club; Visa.
An American-style cocktail/burger restaurant that leads a double life. After dark it's a late-night dance spot; on sunny days its street-side sun lounge is a pleasant place for tea or a snack and their hot dogs, kiddyburgers (free on Sundays) and popular American dishes make ideal fare for children's weekend treats.

Mayfair **Tiddy Dols Eating House**
55 Shepherd Market
London, W1
Tel: 499 2357/8
Buses: 9, 14, 19, 22, 38, 55
Underground: Green Park
Open: 6pm-2am (food served until midnight) every day
Average prices: starters £1.85-£4.25; mains £5.75-£12; puddings £1.25-£2.40; coffee 90p. Children: two-thirds adult prices.
Credit cards: Access; AmEx; Carte Blanche; Diners Club; Luncheon Vouchers; Visa
Tiddy Dols, named after an eccentric eighteenth-century gingerbread maker who had a stall on the site, is an unusual restaurant for a special family evening out. Old English recipes (fisherman's pie, Woodforde's Cornish chicken pasty, blackcurrant fool and trifle) are served here, including various vegetarian and vegan dishes. From 7-11pm every night there's live entertainment in the Music Room, including Classical music, Victorian music hall, the Mayfair Town Crier's original version of the news and acts such as Instant Sunshine of radio and TV fame. Tiddy Dols occupies eight small houses, so there's plenty of room for a quiet meal away from the entertainment and rooms for private parties. Both babies and children are welcomed.

Notting Hill Gate/ **Obelisk**
Paddington 294 Westbourne Grove
London, W11
Tel: 229 1877
Buses: 31
Underground: Notting Hill Gate
Open: noon-11pm Mon-Fri, Sun; 11.30am-11.30pm Sat
Average prices: crêpes 85p-£2.70; galettes 95p-£4; starters £1.10-£1.50; mains: £1.95-£2.25; beverages 30p-£1.85.
Credit cards: Access; Luncheon Vouchers; Visa.
Crêpes (sweet) and galettes (savoury), with a variety of delicate fillings, make ideal lunch or tea-time snacks for children.
Obelisk is one of the original London crêperies. It is a large restaurant on two floors, with round polished table and wooden chairs, pavement tables and a conservatory with doors that open back in summer. There are high chairs for babies and children are especially welcomed.

Surinders Café Brasserie
43 Hereford Road
London, W2
Tel: 221 9192
Buses: 7, 15, 23, 27
Underground: Bayswater, Notting Hill Gate
Open: 9.30am-3.30pm Mon; 9.30am-11.30pm Tue-Sat
Average prices: lunch-time plats du jour £2.50 +VAT; evening menu (three courses including coffee) £7.50 + VAT; snacks 75p-£1.50; cakes 70p, 80p; beverages 40p-90p.
Credit cards: AmEx; Visa.

A delightful neighbourhood café-restaurant run by a group of friends; go for morning coffee, lunch, afternoon tea, a snack or dinner. The emphasis here is on fish dishes, such as bouillabaisse, languoustines or a salmon dish. Ask for a large starter or a small main dish for children if you are having a set meal; the price will be reduced accordingly. The brasserie is on the ground floor, with outdoor tables in summer; downstairs is a space for the arts in which regular events take place, including exhibitions, poetry readings, talks by novelists and some children's events, (such as an exhibition of toys made by children in February, 1985).

Oxford Street
Selfridges Basement Bistro and Top of the Shop
Oxford Street (Close to Baker Street)
London, W1
Tel: 629 1234
Buses: 7, 8, 15, 25, 73
Underground: Marble Arch, Bond Street
Open: 9 am-5.15 pm Mon-Wed, Fri, Sat, 9 am-7.15 pm Thurs
Average prices: Snacks 85p-£5; children's portions £1-£2 in Top of the Shop

Least crowded (usually) and most comfortable of Selfridges' restaurants are the Basement Bistro and Top of the Shop on the 4th floor.

The Basement Bistro can be reached via the little-used entrance and staircase to the west of the main door. The self-service counter has a mini carvery plus a variety of meat dishes such as chilli con carne. The menu includes snacks, such as soup and a roll (95p), and a selection of cakes and puddings. You will usually find spare tables even on Saturdays.

In Top of the Shop which tends to be busier, children can have small portions of their favourites, such as sausages (39p) and fishfingers (28p).

Putney
Bridges
333 Putney Bridge Road
London, SW15 2PG
Tel: 789 2172
Buses: 14, 22, 30, 74, 220
Underground: East Putney, Putney Bridge
Open: noon-3 pm, 6 pm-midnight Mon-Fri; noon-midnight Fri, Sat
Average prices: starters 95p-£1.85; mains £1.95-£5.95; puddings £1.10-£2.70; beverages 40p-£1.25; children's menu £1.25 (one main course)
Credit cards: Access; Diners Club; Luncheon Vouchers; Visa.

An up-market riverside burgers-and-pasta restaurant with a clean and modern – but rather cold – blue and grey décor. Food here is good and the service helpful and pleasant. Prices are low for the Putney area; there is a minimum charge of £2 only after 8 pm and you can go in for morning coffee or cakes and tea at the weekends. Children under 12 may have a burger and chips or spaghetti bolognese for £1.25 and a pudding for half price.

147

Richmond **Haweli**

15-17 Hill Rise
Richmond, Surrey
Tel: 940 3002
Buses: 37, 71, 75
BR station/Underground: Richmond
Open: noon-2pm Mon-Sat, noon-3pm (lunch); 6.30-11pm daily (dinner).
Average prices: starters £1.55-£1.75; mains £3.50-£6.90; puddings £1.40-£1.50; coffee 80p; Sunday buffet £7.50 adults, £3.50 children.
Credit cards: Access; AmEx; Diners Club; Visa.
If you love Indian food and want your children to learn to like it, you will find them welcome and treated indulgently in most Indian restaurants. In most you can order a starter as a children's portion. Take them along to the family buffet lunches served on Sundays in most of the 'new-style' Indian restaurants (recognisable by the absence of flock wallpaper from the décor). The Haweli is a beautifully decorated Indian restaurant serving excellent Mogul dishes from North India and featuring live Indian music at dinner on Fridays and Saturdays. The food here is well known among the affluent, European-born Asian community for the precision of its spicing and high quality. It is especially suitable for children because Mogul dishes, full of cream and almonds, are very mild. The Haweli's Sunday buffet lunches are very good value and children are charged half price; if you're prepared to negotiate a little, they will charge reduced prices for children's portions at other times.

Mrs Beeton's

58 Hill Rise, Richmond
Surrey TW10 6UB
Tel: 940 9561
Buses: 37, 71, 75
BR station/Underground: Richmond
Open: 10am-5pm Mon, Sun; 10am-10.15pm Tue-Sat
Average prices: starters 35p-£1; mains £2.10-£2.40; puddings and cakes 20p-75p; beverages 20p-40p. Unlicensed.
A number of housewives – themselves mothers – run the delightful Mrs Beeton's, close by Richmond Park. A different housewife/chef cooks each daytime and evening session, so the food is basically British, with a few international dishes, and the menu changes twice a day. Some chefs reduce their prices for children, others do not, but prices here are well below average. Go for morning coffee, lunch, tea or an informal dinner. Babies are welcome and although high chairs are not provided, there's plenty of space on the ground floor to park prams; the most comfortable seating is upstairs (note that the toilets are through the antique shop in the basement). A coffee-bar atmosphere, but fast table service and a rapid turnover.

Soho/
Picadilly Circus **Chuen Cheng Ku**

17 Wardour Street
London, W1
Tel: 437 1398

Buses: 14, 19, 22, 38, 55
Underground: Piccadilly Circus
Open: 11am-11.45pm every day
Average prices: dim sum 80p-£2.20; main dishes £2.10-£13.50; set meals: £10.50-£21.
Credit cards: Access; AmEx; Diners Club; Visa.

Babies and children are admitted as a matter of course to all but the most up-market Chinese restaurants, but few have special facilities for children. Chinatown's Chuen Cheng Ku is an exception in that they have two baby chairs, lots of high chairs and an indulgent attitude towards children sharing their parents' dishes. This is a huge Cantonese restaurant decorated with a tall dragon totem pole and serpentine dragons along the walls upstairs, and it boasts one of Chinatown's longest menus. Many children love their superlative dim sum (steamed or fried Chinese dumplings), served before 5pm. Alternatively, order their fish and vegetables in nests, spare ribs in barbecue sauce or sweet and sour dishes.

Mario and Franco's Pizza Pasta Factory

The Trocadero, 7 Rupert Street
London, W1
Tel: 439 8476
Buses: 1, 3, 6, 9, 12, 13, 15, 17, 22, 23, 24, 29, 38, 53, 55, 88, 159, 176
Underground: Leicester Square, Picadilly Circus
Open: noon-midnight every day
Average prices: starters £1.10-£1.80; pizzas £2.15-£5.55; pasta £2.25-£2.75; puddings 90p-£1.15; beverages 40p-£1; children's menu £3.
Credit cards: Access; AmEx; Diners Club; Luncheon Vouchers; Mario & Franco; Visa.

The Pizza Pasta Factory in the Italian Piazza is indubitably the nicest place to eat in the Trocadero. It's busy, but rarely packed and, therefore, convenient if you're shopping in the area or visiting the Guinness Book of Records Exhibition upstairs (take the escalator or a lift to the restaurant on the lower ground floor). Pizzas, pasta and sauces are all freshly made and there's a children's menu of pizza or pasta, ice cream and a fizzy drink. If you're with young children, ask for a baby chair to sit at one of the 'outdoor' tables and park the pushchair alongside your table.

Sydenham ## Mister Moons

82 Sydenham Road
London, SE26
Tel: 659 2030
Buses: 75, 108B, 194, 194A
BR station/Underground: Sydenham
Open: noon-2pm every day (lunch); 7.15-10pm Mon-Thur; 7.15-10.30pm Fri, Sat.
Average prices: £7.50, £8.50, £9, £10, £11.50 plus coffee 65p; children half price.
Credit cards: Access; AmEx; Diners Club; Visa.

Mr Moons is loved in the area for its friendly atmosphere, good food and professional, affable service. The price of the main dish includes a starter, vegetables of the day and a choice of pudding; only wine and coffee are extra. The menu is international and includes dishes such as halibut mornay, pork Havana (flamed in wine with apple purée and finished with cream) veal Cordon Bleu (stuffed with ham and cheese, coated with breadcrumbs and pan fried) and chicken asparagus. Babies and children are welcomed at all meals, except for dinner on Saturdays. At Sunday lunch children often play out in the garden with the proprietor's daughter and her toys while their parents chat over coffee.

Victoria ## Rubens Hotel Carvery

Buckingham Palace Road
London, SW1
Tel: 834 6600
Buses: 38, 55
BR station/Underground: Victoria
Open: 12.30-2.30pm, 6-10pm, every day.
Average prices: set meal £9.25, children under 12 half price Sunday lunch.
Credit cards: Access; AmEx; Carte Blanche; Diners Club; JCB; Trust House Forte; Visa.

Most international hotels have carveries, serving traditional English roast lunches and dinners. These are excellent places for families. The set-price menu (about £9) usually includes a choice of starters, as much roast and veg as you can eat, pudding or cheese and unlimited coffee. Children under 12 are usually charged half price and there is often no charge at all for under-5s. The Carvery at the Rubens Hotel (close to Buckingham Palace and Regent's Park) is spacious and comfortable and there is a small a la carte menu for the more adventurous. There are high chairs for babies and the resident pianist will entertain your children with their favourite tunes on request.

Tootsies

Branches: 115 Notting Hill Gate, W11 (727 6562); 120 Holland Park Avenue, W11 (229 8565); 117 New King's Road, SW6 (735 4023); 140 Fulham Road, SW10 (370 2794)
Open: noon-midnight every day (Notting Hill, Parsons Green) 8am-midnight Mon-Sat; 9am-11.30pm Sunday (Holland Park, Fulham Road). (Bookings accepted for children's parties only.)
Average prices: hamburgers £1.95-£2.90; salads 95p-£2.95; specialities £1.95-£6.95; puddings 90p-£1.50; beverages 45p-60p; children's menu £1.50 (one main course).
Credit cards: Luncheon vouchers only

Relaxed, informal eating is the keynote of this small chain of burger restaurants aimed at Londoners, rather than tourists. Feel free to linger over your meal. The 'Tootsies Tots' menu for under tens, available at all branches, gives a choice between a small hamburger, half a bun, chips and beans or a fried egg or a mini portion of bangers 'n' mash with beans. In addition, the Fulham Road and Parsons Green restaurants provide bibs and baby booster seats and will arrange children's birthday parties (minimum 15 people, book in advance). These include a conjuror or Punch and Judy show, as many hamburgers, chips, ice creams and milk shakes as the guests can manage, a personalised birthday cake, hats, balloons and novelties. The parties are supervised but parents can hang around and watch.

Grateful acknowledgement is made to Helen Varley, Editor of the *Time Out* Restaurant Guide *Eating Out in London* for compiling this restaurant section.

DIRECTORY

Art Galleries

The Iveagh Bequest
Kenwood
Hampstead Lane
London NW3 7JR
Tel: 01-348 1286
Opening times: April to September: daily 10.00am-7.00pm;
February, March and October: daily 10.00am-5.00pm;
November to January: 10.00am-4.00pm
Admission: free
Buses: 210
Underground: Archway, Golders Green
Large collection of 18th-century English paintings. Children's
workshop, with painting, acting and
worksheets, held over Christmas and New Year. See walk 13.

Leighton House Museum and Art Gallery
12 Holland Park Road
London W14 8LZ
Tel: 01-602 3316
Opening times: Mondays to Saturdays 9.00am-5.00pm; closed
Bank Holidays
Admission: free
Buses: 9, 28, 33, 49, 73
BR station: Victoria
Underground: High Street Kensington, Holland Park
High Victorian house built by the artist Lord Leighton, with
magnificent Arab Hall with hundreds of tiles, and wooden
screens. Collection of paintings and drawings by Lord Leighton.

The National Gallery
Trafalgar Square
London WC2N 5DN
Tel: 01-839 3321
Opening times: Mondays to Saturdays 10.00am-6.00pm;
Sundays 2.00-6.00pm
Admission: free
Buses: 1, 3, 6, 9, 11, 12, 13, 15, 23, 24, 29, 53, 77, 77A, 88, 159,
168, 170, 176, 500
BR station: Charing Cross
Underground: Charing Cross, Leicester Square
Old Master Paintings from Britain and Europe, $c.1250$-$c.1900$.
Worksheets, talks, guided tours and holiday events.

National Portrait Gallery
St Martin's Place
London WC2
Tel: 01-930 1552
Opening times: Mondays to Fridays 10.00 am-5.00 pm;
Saturdays 10.00 am-6.00 pm; Sundays 2.00-6.00 pm; closed some
Bank Holidays
Admission: free
Buses: 1, 3, 6, 9, 11, 12, 13, 15, 24, 29, 53, 77, 77A, 88, 159, 168,
170, 176
BR station: Charing Cross
Underground: Charing Cross, Embankment, Leicester Square
National museum of portraits, arranged in chronological order
and grouped according to theme. Children's holiday activities
three times a year, including practical workshops.

Ranger's House
Chesterfield House
Blackheath
London SE10
Tel: 01-853 0035
Opening times: February to October: daily 10.00 am-5.00 pm;
November to January: daily 10.00 am-4.00 pm
Admission: free
Buses: 53, 54, 75
BR station: Blackheath
Elizabethan and Jacobean portraits in full-length costume.

Sir John Soane's Museum
13 Lincoln's Inn Fields
London WC2A 3BP
Tel: 01-405 2107
Opening times: Tuesdays to Saturdays 10.00 am-5.00 pm
Admission: free
Buses: 7, 25, 68, 77A, 501, 502
Underground: Holborn
Houses belonging to the architect Sir John Soane and containing
his fabulous collection of paintings, relics, furniture, etc.
See walk 6.

The Tate Gallery
Millbank
London SW1P 4RG
Tel: 01-821 1313; recorded information on 01-821 7128
Opening times: Mondays to Saturdays 10.00 am-5.50 pm;
Sundays 2.00-5.50 pm; closed some Bank Holidays
Admission: free
Buses: 77A, 88

BR station: Vauxhall
Underground: Pimlico
British paintings, sculpture, watercolours, drawings and
engravings from the 16th century onwards; modern painting (from
the late 19th century onwards) from throughout the world; prints
by British and foreign artists. Seasonal trails, competitions and
guided tours.

Arts Workshops

Albany Empire
Douglas Way
Deptford
London SE8
Tel: 01-691 8016
Membership: 50p a night, £1.00 for four months, £2.50 a year
Buses: 1, 47, 53, 177
BR station: Deptford, New Cross
Underground: New Cross
Theatre workshops.

Barnet Arts Workshop
Avenue House
East End Road
Finchley Central
London N3 3QF
Tel: 01-346 7120
Buses: 143
Underground: Finchley Central
Regular evening and holiday activities in drama, dance, visual arts,
etc.

Battersea Arts Centre
Old Town Hall
Lavender Hill
London SW11
Tel: 01-223 6557
Membership: £7.50 a year, adults only
Buses: 19, 37, 39, 45, 77, 77A, 170, 249
BR station: Clapham Junction
Film and theatre performance workshops, ballet and guitar
workshops; shows for under 5s in holiday periods. Half-term
projects incorporating costume-making, photography, theatre and
dance, culminating in a performance at the end of the week.
Residential Youth Dance Weekend during the annual dance
festival in early July.

Camden Arts Centre
Arkwright Road
London NW3 6DG
Tel: 01-435 2643; 01-435 5224
Buses: 2, 13, 113
BR station: Finchley Road and Frognal
Underground: Finchley Road, Hampstead
Weekend classes throughout the year, and classes each school
holiday on all aspects of the visual arts.

Lauderdale Community Arts Centre
Lauderdale House
Waterlow Park
Highgate Hill
London N6 5HG
Tel: 01-348 8716
Buses: 143, 210, 271
Underground: Archway
Regular after-school workshops in drama, dance and the visual
arts.

Lewisham Academy of Music
77 Watson's Street
Deptford
London SE8
Tel: 01-691 0307
Membership: 60p a month
Music workshops.

Lyric Theatre
King Street
Hammersmith
London W6
Tel: 01-741 2311 (box office); 01-741 0824 (administration)
Buses: 27, 91, 267
Underground: Hammersmith
Workshop classes in basic theatre skills.

Old Bull Arts Centre
68 High Street
Barnet
Hertfordshire
Tel: 01-449 5189
Admission: 75p for workshops
Buses: 26, 34, 84A, 107, 134, 263
BR station: New Barnet

155

Underground: High Barnet
Regular classes and workshops on drama, art, crafts, dance and
half-term and summer activities.

Oval House Community Arts Centre
52-54 Kennington Oval
London SE11 5SW
Tel: 01-582 7680 (box office); 01-735 2786
(administration)
Buses: 3, 36, 36A, 109, 133, 155, 159
BR station: Vauxhall
Underground: Oval
Wide variety of classes and workshops for all ages, some of which
lead to productions in the theatre.

Polka Children's Theatre
240 The Broadway
Wimbledon
London SW19 1SB
Tel: 01-543 4888 (box office); 01-542 4258 (administration)
Buses: 57, 93, 155, 293
BR station: Wimbledon
Underground: South Wimbledon, Wimbledon
Regular craft workshops in craft and drama, including music and
puppetry, mime, circus skills, story-telling, dance, face-painting
and masks, held after school and during school holidays. Details
available via mailing list.

Queens' Theatre
Billet Lane
Hornchurch
Essex
RM11 1ET
Tel: 04024-4333 (box office); 04024-56118 (administration)
Admission: children £2.10-£2.40, adults £3.30-£4.80
Buses: 193, 226, 246, 248, 256, 294, 370, 371
BR stations: Emerson Park, Romford
Underground: Hornchurch
Youth drama company.

Riverside Studios
Crisp Road
Hammersmith
London W6 9RL
Tel: 01-748 3354 (box office); 01-741 2251 (administration)

156

Buses: 9, 9A, 11, 33, 73, 220, 266, 267, 290
Underground: Hammersmith
Half-term workshops with visual artists, summer dance courses, and theatre classes.

Sadler's Wells Theatre Community Development

Rosebery Avenue
London EC1R 4TN
Tel: 01-278 6563 extension 23
Admission: children 50p-£1.50, adults £1.00-£2.00
Buses: 19, 30, 38, 171
BR stations: King's Cross, St Pancras
Underground: Angel
Workshops with visiting companies, school holiday events, open rehearsals, backstage visits and tours.

Secombe Centre

Cheam Road
Sutton
Surrey
SM1 2ST
Tel: 01-661 0416
Buses: 93, 213, 408
BR station: Sutton
Regular school holiday activities; weekly drama classes.

Tom Allen Community Arts Centre

Grove Crescent Road
Stratford
London E15
Tel: 01-555 7289
Membership: 50p a year
Admission: free to many events; children 50p-£1.40, adults £2.00-£2.75
Buses: 10, 51, 69, 86, 173, 212, 225, 238, 241, 262, 278
BR station: Stratford
Underground: Stratford
Free weekly children's drama workshop for 6-12 year olds; regular half-term and holiday events, e.g. art and print workshops.

Unicorn Children's Theatre

6-7 Great Newport Street
London WC2
Tel: 01-836 3334 (box office); 01-379 3280 (theatre club)
Membership: £3.00-£15.00

Buses: 1, 24, 29, 176
BR station: Charing Cross
Underground: Leicester Square
Thriving theatre club which holds regular drama workshops based
on themes from stories, arts and crafts workshops on topics such
as masks, puppets, scene-painting and collage, and skill
workshops on the technical side of drama.

Watermans Arts Centre
40 High Street
Brentford
Middlesex
Tel: 01-568 3312
Buses: 27, 65, 237, 267
BR stations: Brentford, Kew Bridge
Underground: Gunnersbury, South Ealing
Regular classes in drama, writing, storytelling, dance, etc.

Astronomy

London Planetarium
Marylebone Road
London NW1 5LR
Tel: 01-486 1121
Opening times: daily 11.00 am-4.30 pm
30-minute shows given regularly throughout the day
Admission: children £1.20, adults £1.80; combined ticket with
Madame Tussaud's next door, children £2.55, adults £4.45
Buses: 2, 13, 18, 27, 30, 113, 159, 176
BR station: Euston, Marylebone, Paddington
Underground: Baker Street
30-minute star show under the dome, and exhibition 'The
Astronomers' Gallery'.
See walk 9.

Old Royal Observatory
Greenwich Park
Greenwich
London SE10
Tel: 01-858 4422
Opening times: summer: Mondays to Saturdays
10.00 am-6.00 pm, Sundays 2.00-5.00 pm; winter: Mondays to
Fridays 10.00 am-5.00 pm, Saturdays 10.00 am-5.30 pm, Sundays
2.00-5.00 pm; closed some Bank Holidays

Admission: children 75p, adults £1.50
Buses: 108B, 177, 185, 188
BR stations: Greenwich, Maze Hill
The original Royal Observatory, with astronomical equipment;
Greenwich Meridian.
See walk 12.

Brass Rubbing

All Hallows Church by the Tower
Byward Street
London EC4
Tel: 01-481 2928
Opening times: Mondays to Saturdays 11.00 am-5.45 pm;
Sundays 12.30-5.45 pm
Charge: varies according to brass rubbed
Buses: 23, 42, 56, 78
BR station: Fenchurch Street
Underground: Tower Hill
Replicas of more than 20 brasses.

London Brass Rubbing Centre
St James's Church
Piccadilly
London W1
Tel: 01-437 6023
Opening times: Mondays to Saturdays 10.00 am-6.00 pm;
Sundays 12.00-6.00 pm
Charge: Varies according to brass rubbed
Buses: 3, 6, 9, 12, 13, 14, 15, 19, 22, 23, 38, 53, 55, 88, 159
BR station: Charing Cross
Underground: Piccadilly Circus
Replicas of more than 60 brasses, mostly from Britain but some
from abroad.

Caves

Chislehurst Caves
Old Hill
Chislehurst
Kent
Tel: 01-467 3264
Opening times: 1st day of Easter Holidays to 30 September:
guided tours daily from 11.00 am-5.00 pm; 1 October to end of

spring term: Sundays only 11.00am-5.00pm
Admission: children 50p, adults £1.00
Buses: 227, 725 (Green Line)
BR station: Chislehurst
Miles of historic caves, parts of which date from the Stone Age;
fossils; Dr Who Cave; Caves' Witch.

Cemeteries

Highgate Cemetery
Swains Lane
London N6 6PJ
Tel: 01-340 1834
Opening times: guided tours daily on the hour: April to
September 10.00am-4.00pm; October to March
10.00am-3.00pm; four special open days a year
Buses: 53, 214
BR station: Gospel Oak
Underground: Archway
Enormous overgrown Victorian cemetery.
See walk 13.

Nunhead Cemetery
London SE
Tel: 01-732 7360; 01-639 1613
Opening times: The Friends of Nunhead Cemetery holds
conducted tours on the last Sunday of every month. Meet at
2.15pm at the Linden Grove entrance.
Admission: free

Cinemas

Battersea Arts Centre
Old Town Hall
Lavender Hill
London SW11
Tel: 01-223 6557
Opening times: Saturdays and Sundays at 3.30pm
Admission: Saturdays 75p, adults £1.50+ membership; Sundays
£1.00, adults £1.60+ membership
Buses: 19, 37, 39, 45, 77, 77A, 170, 249
BR station: Clapham Junction

Children's Cinema Club
The Barbican Centre
London EC2Y 8DS
Tel: 01-636 8891; 01-628 8795
Opening times: Saturdays at 11.00am and 2.30pm
Membership: £1.00 a year, 50p a day
Admission: £1.00 per member, adults £1.50
Buses: 4, 8, 9, 11, 21, 23, 25, 43, 76, 104, 133, 141, 214, 271
BR stations: Barbican, Broad Street, Cannon Street, Holborn
Viaduct, Liverpool Street, Moorgate
Underground: Bank, Barbican, Liverpool Street, Moorgate,
St Paul's
Films and cartoons for 6-12 year olds; adults not allowed unless
accompanied by a child.

National Film Theatre
South Bank
Waterloo
London SE1 8XT
Tel: 01-928 3232 (box office); 01-633 0274 (ticket availability
information)
Admission: children £1.25, adults £2.50
Buses: 1, 4, 5, 68, 70, 149, 171, 176, 188, 501, 502, 507, 513
BR station: Waterloo
Underground: Waterloo
Weekend screenings of films under the title Junior NFT, usually
for 3-month season with a related theme. Membership fees are
waived, but children must be accompanied by an adult. Films in
regular monthly programme thought suitable for children are
marked (J).

Wandsworth Film Club
York Gardens Community Centre
Lavender Road
London SW11
Tel: 01-233 7961
Opening times: Friday at 5.00pm except during school holidays
Admission: children 40p, adults 80p
Buses: 37, 44, 45, 77
BR station: Clapham Junction
Occasional film-making workshops for children.

Watermans Arts Centre
40 High Street
Brentford
Middlesex
Tel: 01-568 3312
Buses: 27, 65, 237, 267

BR stations: Brentford, Kew Bridge
Underground: Gunnersbury, South Ealing
Regular summer holiday films.

Commercial and Financial Institutions

London International Financial Futures Exchange
Royal Exchange
London EC3V 3PJ
Tel: 01-623 0444
Opening times: Mondays to Fridays 11.45 am-2.00 pm; closed Bank Holidays
Admission: free
Buses: 6, 8, 9, 11, 15, 21, 22, 25, 43, 76, 133, 149, 501
BR station: Cannon Street
Underground: Bank
The Visitors' Gallery overlooks the floor of the Exchange.

Stock Exchange
London EC2 1HP
(entrance to Visitors' Gallery in Old Broad Street)
Tel: 01-588 2355
Opening times: Mondays to Fridays 9.45 am-3.15 pm; closed Bank Holidays
Admission: free
Buses: 9, 11, 279A, 502
BR stations: Broad Street, Liverpool Street
Underground: Bank, Liverpool Street
Talks and film shows are held daily at 10.00 am, 10.30 am, 11.30 am, 12.30 pm, 1.30 pm and 2.30 pm. The Visitors' Gallery overlooks the floor of the Stock Exchange.

Ice-Skating

Lea Valley Ice Centre
Lea Bridge Road
Leyton
London E10 7QL
Tel: 01-533 3151

Opening times: daily 10.00am-12.00pm, 2.00-4.00pm, 7.30 or
8.30-10.30pm (except Sundays)
Admission: £1.20-£2.40 per session
Buses: 38, 48, 55
BR station: Clapton
Underground: Blackhorse Road, Leyton

Queen's Ice Skating Club
17 Queensway
London W2
Tel: 01-229 0172
Opening times: daily 10.00am-12.00pm, 2.00-5.00pm,
7.00-10.00pm
Admission: 90p-£3.20 per session
Buses: 12, 88
BR station: Paddington
Underground: Queensway

Richmond Ice Rink
Clevedon Road
Twickenham
Middlesex TW1 2HX
Tel: 01-892 3646
Opening times: public skating daily 10.00am-12.30pm,
2.30-5.00pm, 7.30-10.00pm
Admission: £1.20-£2.10 per session
Buses: 33, 37, 202, 270, 290
BR station: Richmond
Underground: Richmond

Streatham Ice Rink
386 Streatham High Road
London SW16 6HT
Tel: 01-769 7861/2
Opening times: Mondays to Fridays 10.00am-12.30pm,
2.00-4.30pm, 8.00-10.30pm; Wednesdays also 4.00-5.00pm,
Fridays also 3.45-4.45pm ("after school" sessions); Saturdays
10.00am-12.30pm, 2.30-5.00pm, 8.00-10.30pm; Sundays
10.00am-12.30pm, 2.30-5.00pm, 9.00-11.00pm
Admission: 80p-£2.20 per session
Buses: 49, 50, 109, 133, 159, 181, 249
BR station: Streatham

Lectures and Talks

British Library Exhibition Galleries
British Museum
Great Russell Street
London WC1B 3DG
Tel: 01-636 1544
Admission: free
Buses: 5, 7, 8, 19, 22, 25, 38, 55, 68, 77A, 153, 172, 188, 501
BR stations: Charing Cross, Euston
Underground: Holborn, Russell Square, Tottenham Court Road
Regular programme of gallery talks, lectures and audio-visual presentations on English writers, medieval and Anglo-Saxon manuscripts, Indian manuscripts, Persian, Turkish and Mogul painting.

Geological Museum
Exhibition Road
London SW7
Tel: 01-589 3456
Admission: free
Buses: 9, 14, 30, 33, 45, 49, 52, 52A, 73, 74
BR station: Victoria
Underground: South Kensington
Occasional public lectures on topics such as volcanoes, earthquakes, etc.

Molecule Theatre of Science
Mermaid Theatre
Puddle Dock
Blackfriars
London EC4
Tel: 01-236 9521 extension 259
Admission: children 50p, adults £1.00
Buses: 45, 63, 76, 109, 141, 184
BR station: Blackfriars
Underground: Blackfriars, St Paul's
Molecule Discussions, occasional series of illustrated lectures for 13-18 year olds given by eminent scientists; scientific adventure plays for 4-11 year olds also staged.

Science Museum
Exhibition Road
London SW7
Tel: 01-589 3456

Admission: free
Buses: 9, 14, 30, 33, 45, 49, 52, 52A, 73, 74
BR station: Victoria
Underground: North Kensington
30-minute lectures on most Tuesdays and Thursdays at 1.00pm
on particular collections in the museum, sometimes accompanied
by demonstrations. 60-minute lectures on Saturdays at 3.00pm on
a scientific or technological subject, illustrated by a full range of
demonstrations. Special Christmas lectures also given.

General Museums

Commonwealth Institute
Kensington High Street
London W8
Tel: 01-603 4535
Opening times: Mondays to Saturdays 10.00am-5.30pm;
Sundays 2.00-5.00pm; closed some Bank Holidays
Admission: free
Buses: 9, 27, 28, 31, 33, 49, 73
BR station: Paddington
Underground: High Street Kensington
Exhibition on the culture, lifestyle and resources of the 40-plus
countries of the Commonwealth. Art Gallery and theatre/cinema.

Fenton House
Hampstead Grove
Hampstead
London NW3
Tel: 01-435 3471
Opening times: March: Saturdays and Sundays only
2.00-6.00pm; April to October: daily except Thursdays and
Fridays 11.00am-6.00pm; last admission 1 hour before closing
time
Admission: children 85p, adults £1.70
Buses: 210, 268
Underground: Hampstead
Attractive late 17th-century house with collections of furniture,
porcelain and musical instruments.
See walk 13.

Guinness World of Records
The Trocadero
Piccadilly
London W1V 7FD
Tel: 01-439 7331

Opening times: daily 10.00 am-10.00 pm
Admission: children £1.50, adults £2.50
Buses: 3, 6, 9, 12, 13, 14, 15, 19, 22, 23, 38, 53, 55, 88, 159
BR station: Charing Cross
Underground: Piccadilly Circus
Exhibition based on the *Guinness Book of Records*, covering the
following themes: the human world, the animal world, our planet
Earth, structures and machines, the sports world, the world of
entertainment, British innovation and achievement.

Horniman Museum & Library

London Road
Forest Hill
London SE23 3PQ
Tel: 01-699 2339; 01-600 1872; 01-699 4911
Opening times: Mondays to Saturdays 10.30 am-6.00 pm;
Sundays 2.00-6.00 pm
Admission: free
Buses: 12, 12A, 63, 122, 124, 171, 185, 194, P4
BR station: Forest Hill
Extensive ethnographic, natural history and musical instrument
collections. Aspects of the culture of Africa, the Americas, the
Pacific, the Far East and Ancient Egypt. Folk instruments,
oriental art instruments and European instruments.

Museum of Mankind

6 Burlington Gardens
London W1X 2EX
Tel: 01-437 2224
Opening times: Mondays to Saturdays 10.00 am-5.00 pm;
Sundays 2.30-6.00 pm; closed some Bank Holidays
Admission: free
Buses: 3, 6, 9, 9A, 12, 13, 14, 15, 19, 19A, 22, 38, 39, 53, 55, 59,
88, 159
BR station: Charing Cross
Underground: Green Park, Piccadilly
Extensive collections from non-Western cultures, including
Africa, North and South America, parts of Asia and Europe, and
Australia and the Pacific Islands. Worksheets, some handling
sessions during school holidays, film shows.
See walk 4.

Musical Museum

368 Brentford High Street
Middlesex TW8 0BD
Tel: 01-560 8108
Opening times: April to October: Saturdays and Sundays
2.00-5.00 pm; closed Bank Holidays

Buses: 65, 237, 267
BR station: Kew Bridge
Underground: Gunnersbury
Large collection of automatic musical instruments, including reproducing piano systems, and pipe organs, (including giant Wurlitzer).
See walk 13.

National Postal Museum
King Edward Building
King Edward Street
London EC1A 1LP
Tel: 01-432 3851; 01-606 3769
Opening times: Mondays to Thursdays 10.00 am-4.30 pm; Fridays 10.00 am-4.00 pm; closed Bank Holidays
Admission: free
Buses: 8, 22, 25
BR stations: Holborn Viaduct, Moorgate
Underground: Barbican, Moorgate, St Paul's
Stamps from throughout the world, with special emphasis on British and Commonwealth; Penny Blacks.
See walk 8.

The Scout Association
Baden-Powell House
Queen's Gate
London SW7 5JS
Tel: 01-584 7030
Opening times: Mondays to Fridays 9.00 am-5.00 pm
Admission: free
Buses: 49, 74
BR stations: Paddington, Victoria
Underground: Gloucester Road, South Kensington
The Baden-Powell story, and the history of the Scout and Girl Guide Movements. Quiz sheet.

Historical Museums

British Library Exhibition Galleries
British Museum
Great Russell Street
London WC1B 3DG
Tel: 01-636 1544
Opening times: Mondays to Saturdays 10.00 am-5.00 pm; Sundays 2.30-6.00 pm; closed some Bank Holidays
Admission: free
Buses: 5, 7, 8, 19, 22, 25, 38, 55, 68, 77A, 153, 188, 501

BR stations: Charing Cross, Euston
Underground: Holborn, Russell square, Tottenham Court Road
The British Library's exhibition galleries are housed in the British
Museum. Treasures on display include Magna Carta, the
Lindisfarne Gospels, Shakespeare's first folios, the Gutenberg
Bible.

King Henry VIII Wine Cellar
Horse Guards
Whitehall
London SW1
Opening times: April to September: Saturdays 2.30-4.30 pm
Admission: free
Buses: 3, 11, 12, 24, 29, 53, 70, 77, 77A, 88, 109, 159, 170, 184
BR station: Charing Cross
Underground: Embankment, Westminster
Applications in advance and in writing to:
Room 10/14
St Christopher House
Southwark Street
London SE1 0TE
Only surviving remains of York Palace, Cardinal Wolsey's London
house, later converted by Henry VIII into Whitehall Palace. The
Wine Cellar is in the foundations of the Ministry of Defence
building.
See walk 2.

Tower of London
Tower Hill
London EC3N 4AB
Tel: 01-709 0765
Opening times: March to October: Mondays to Saturdays
9.30 am-5.45 pm, Sundays 2.00-5.45 pm; November to February:
Mondays to Saturdays 9.30 am-4.30 pm; last admission
45 minutes before closing time in summer, 30 minutes in winter;
closed some Bank Holidays
Admission: March to October: children £1.50, adults £3.00;
November to February: children £1.00, adults £2.00
Buses: 23, 42, 56, 78
BR station: Fenchurch Street
Underground: Tower Hill
Royal fortress since the 11th century; tower armouries and Crown
Jewels. Heralds Museum.

Wellington Museum
Apsley House
49 Piccadilly
Hyde Park Corner
London W1V 9FA

Tel: 01-499 5676
Opening times: Tuesdays, Wednesdays, Thursdays and
Saturdays 10.00am-6.00pm; Sundays 2.30-6.00pm; closed Bank
Holidays
Admission: children 30p, adults 60p
Buses: 9, 14, 19, 22, 30, 52, 52A, 55, 73, 74, 137, 500
BR station: Victoria
Underground: Hyde Park Corner
London residence of the Duke of Wellington, containing
Wellington relics, paintings, silver plate and porcelain.
See walk 1.

Horror Museums

The London Dungeon
28/34 Tooley Street
London SE1 2SZ
Tel: 01-403 0606
Opening times: April to September: daily 10.00am-5.30pm;
October to March: daily 10.00am-4.30pm
Admission: children £2.00, adults £3.50
Buses: 8A, 10, 18, 21, 35, 40, 43, 44, 47, 48, 70, 133, 501, 513,
P3
BR station: London Bridge
Underground: London Bridge
Lifelike tableaux with dramatic lighting and eerie sound effects
portraying the darker side of medieval history. Not for the
squeamish!
See walk 6.

Literary Museums

Dickens House
48 Doughty Street
London WC1N 2LF
Tel: 01-405 2127
Opening times: Mondays to Saturdays 10.00am-5.00pm; closed
Bank Holidays
Admission: children 50p, adults £1.00
Buses: 5, 17, 18, 19, 38, 46, 55, 171
BR stations: King's Cross, St Pancras
Underground: Holborn, Russell Square
House in which Charles Dickens lived from 1837 to 1839, during
which he secured his reputation as a writer. Reconstructed
drawing-room; manuscripts, letters, first editions, pictures, books,
memorabilia. Worksheets.

Keats House
Wentworth Place
Keats Grove
Hampstead
London NW3 2RR
Tel: 01-435 2062
Opening times: daily 10.00 am-1.00 pm, 2.00-6.00 pm; closed
some Bank Holidays
Buses: 24, 46, 268, C11
BR station: Hampstead Heath
Underground: Belsize Park, Hampstead
Keats's home for the last two years of his life. The sitting-room is
practically unchanged and there are manuscripts, paintings and
memorabilia.
See walk 13.

Museums of London Life

Bear Gardens Museum of the Shakespearean Stage
1 Bear Gardens
Bankside
London SE1 9EB
Tel: 01-928 6342
Opening times: Tuesdays to Saturdays 10.00 am-5.30 pm;
Sundays 2.00-6.00 pm
Admission: children 50p, adults £1.00
Buses: 35, 40, 45, 70, 76
BR stations: Blackfriars, Cannon Street, London Bridge
Underground: Blackfriars, London Bridge, Mansion House
Models and pictures of stage and theatre 1576-1642; working
replica of a 1616 stage.
See walk 6.

Church Farm House Museum
Greyhound Hill
Hendon
London NW4 4JR
Tel: 01-203 0130
Opening times: Mondays and Wednesdays to Saturdays
10.00 am-1.00 pm, 2.00-5.30 pm; Tuesdays 10.00 am-1.00 pm;
Sundays 2.00-5.30 pm; closed some Bank Holidays
Admission: free
Buses: 113, 143, 183, 240
BR station: Hendon
Underground: Hendon Central

170

Museum is housed in a 17th-century farmhouse. There are two
period furnished rooms, a kitchen *c.*1820 and dining-room *c.*1850.
Some six different exhibitions are staged each year.

Cuming Museum
155-157 Walworth Road
London SE17 1RS
Tel: 01-703 3324; 01-703 5529; 01-703 6514
Opening times: Mondays to Fridays 10.00am-5.30pm;
Thursdays to 7.00pm; Saturdays 10.00am-5.00pm; closed Bank
Holidays
Admission: free
Buses: 12, 34, 40, 45, 68, 171, 176, 184
Underground: Elephant and Castle
BR station: Elephant and Castle
Collection concentrates on archaeology of Southwark and on
London superstitions; objects of special interest include Roman
skull, 18th-century dress, performing bear and milk delivery cans.

Epping Forest Museum
Queen Elizabeth's Hunting Lodge
Rangers Road
Chingford
London E4 7QH
Tel: 01-529 6681
Opening times: Wednesdays to Sundays and Bank Holiday
Mondays 2.00-6.00pm; closes at dusk in winter
Admission: children free, adults 25p
Buses: 97, 97A, 102, 179
BR station: Chingford
Specimens of Epping Forest flora and fauna, old traps and
hunting weapons. The museum is housed in a Tudor hunting
grandstand.

Grange Museum of Local History
Neasden Lane
London NW10 1QB
Tel: 01-452 8311
Opening times: Mondays to Fridays 12.00-5.00pm,
Wednesdays until 8.00pm; Saturdays 10.00am-5.00pm; closed
Bank Holidays
Admission: free
Buses: 16, 52, 112, 245, 297
BR station: Brondesbury
Underground: Neasden
Everyday items illustrating the life of the Brent area. Quizzes,
especially in school holidays.

Guildhall
PO Box 270
London EC2P 2EJ
Tel: 01-606 3030
Opening times: Mondays to Saturdays 10.00 am-5.00 pm,
Sundays (May to September) 10.00 am-5.00 pm; closed Bank
Holidays
Clock Museum open Mondays to Fridays 9.30 am-5.00 pm
Admission: free
Buses: 9, 11, 21, 43, 76, 133, 141, 279A, 502
BR station: Cannon Street
Underground: Bank, Mansion House, Moorgate
The Guildhall has been the centre of the City's civic government
for over 1,000 years. Tours by application to City Guide, Public
Relations Office, Guildhall.
See walk 7.

Gunnersbury Park Museum
Gunnersbury Park
London W3 8LQ
Tel: 01-992 1612
Opening times: March to October: Mondays to Fridays
1.00-5.00 pm, Saturdays, Sundays and Bank Holidays 2.00-
6.00 pm; November to February: Mondays to Fridays 1.00-
4.00 pm, Saturdays, Sundays and Bank Holidays 2.00-4.00 pm
Admission: free
Buses: 7, E3
BR station: Gunnersbury
Underground: Acton Town
Local history, including archaeology, transport, domestic life,
trades, crafts, industries, costumes, toys and dolls.

The Monument
Monument Street
London EC3R 8AH
Tel: 01-626 2717
Opening times: 1 April to 30 September: Mondays to Fridays
9.00 am-6.00 pm, Saturdays and Sundays 2.00-6.00 pm;
1 October to 31 March: Mondays to Saturdays 9.00 am-2.00 pm
and 3.00-4.00 pm, closed Sundays; last admission 20 minutes
before closing time
Admission: children 25p, adults 50p
Buses: 8A, 10, 35, 40, 40A, 44, 47, 48
BR station: Cannon Street, London Bridge
Underground: Bank, Monument
See walk 7.

Museum of London
London Wall
London EC2 5HN

Tel: 01-600 3699
Opening times: Tuesdays to Saturdays 10.00 am-6.00 pm;
Sundays 2.00-6.00 pm
Admission: free
Buses: 4, 8, 22, 25, 41, 279A, 501, 502
BR stations: Holborn Viaduct, Liverpool Street, Moorgate
Underground: Bank, Barbican, Moorgate, St Paul's
The museum of London life, with a comprehensive collection
about London from the earliest times to the present day. Essential
visiting.

Orpington Museum
The Priory
Church Hill
Orpington
Kent BR6 0HH
Tel: Orpington (66) 31551 extension 9
Opening times: Mondays to Wednesdays and Fridays
9.00 am-6.00 pm; Saturdays 9.00 am-5.00 pm; closed Thursdays
and Bank Holidays
Admission: free
Buses: 61, 208, 261
BR stations: Orpington, St Mary Cray
Local archaeology from Palaeolithic Age to Roman times. Objects
from Saxon period and from 16th to early 20th centuries. Small
sections on geology and ethnography.

Passmore Edwards Museum
Romford Road
Stratford
London E15 4LZ
Tel: 01-519 4296
Opening times: Mondays to Fridays 10.00 am-6.00 pm;
Saturdays 10.00 am-1.00 pm, 2.00-5.00 pm; Sundays and Bank
Holidays 2.00-5.00 pm
Admission: free
Buses: 25, 86, 225
BR station: Stratford
Underground: Stratford
Local history and archaeology, natural history and geology of
geographical county of Essex (which includes north-east London).
Competition sheets during school holidays.

St Bride's Church and Crypt Museum
Fleet Street
London EC4Y 8AV
Tel: 01-353 1301
Opening times: Mondays to Saturdays 9.00 am-5.00 pm;

Sundays 9.00 am-7.30 pm
Admission: free
Buses: 4, 6, 9, 11, 15, 23, 77, 171, 502, 513
BR station: Blackfriars
Underground: Blackfriars
Museum covers 2,000 years of the site, including Roman and
Celtic remains.
See walk 5.

Tower Bridge
London SE1 2UP
Tel: 01-403 5386 (tourist office); 01-403 3761; 01-407 0922
Opening times: 1 April to 31 October: daily 10.00 am-6.30 pm;
1 November to 31 March: daily 10.00 am-4.45 pm; last admission
45 minutes before closing time; closed some Bank Holidays
Admission: children £1.00, adults £2.00
Buses: 23, 42, 56, 78
BR stations: Fenchurch Street, London Bridge
Underground: London Bridge, Tower Hill
History of the bridge, walkways above and hydraulic lifting
machinery.
See walk 6.

Vestry House Museum
Vestry Road
Walthamstow
London E17 9NH
Tel: 01-527 5544 extension 4391
Opening times: Mondays to Fridays 10.00 am-5.30 pm;
Saturdays 10.00 am-5.00 pm; closed between 1.00 and 2.00 pm
Wednesdays and Saturdays; closed Bank Holidays
Admission: free
Buses: 69, 97, 97A, 212, 275
BR station: Walthamstow Central
Underground: Walthamstow Central
Local history, Victorian domestic life with reconstructed Victorian
parlour, archaeology, costumes, crafts and industry. Victorian
police cell and the Bremer car, reputedly the first British-built
four-wheeled internal combustion engine. The museum is housed
in the 18th-century parish workhouse, later used as a police
station.

Whitehall
1 Malden Road
Cheam
Sutton
Surrey
Tel: 01-643 1236

174

Opening times: April to October: Tuesdays to Fridays, Sundays and Bank Holiday Mondays 2.00-5.30pm, Saturdays 10.00am-5.30pm; November to March: Wednesdays, Thursdays and Sundays 2.00-5.30pm, Saturdays 10.00am-5.30pm; closed some Bank Holidays
Admission: children 25p, adults 50p
Buses: 151, 213, 403, 408, 796
BR station: Cheam
16th-century timber-framed building with later additions. Displays of material from the excavation of Nonsuch Palace nearby.

Medical Museums

Old Operating Theatre and Herb Garret
Guy's Hospital
St Thomas Street
London SE1 9RT
The entrance is via the Chapter House in St Thomas Street.
Tel: 01-407 7600 extension 2739 or 3149
Opening times: Mondays, Wednesdays and Fridays 12.30-4.00pm; closed Bank Holidays
Admission: children 20p, adults 40p
Buses: 8A, 10, 18, 21, 35, 40, 43, 44, 47, 48, 70, 133, 501, 513, P3
BR station: London Bridge
Underground: London Bridge
Original mid-19th century female operating theatre, restored to its original condition, and herb garret used for storing and drying medicinal herbs.
See walk 6.

Science Museum
Exhibition Road
London SW7
Tel: 01-589 3456
Opening times: Mondays to Saturdays 10.00am-6.00pm; Sundays 2.30-6.00pm; closed some Bank Holidays
Admission: free
Buses: 9, 14, 30, 33, 45, 49, 52, 52A, 73, 74
BR station: Victoria
Underground: South Kensington
Includes Wellcome Collection, with re-creations of episodes from medical history and displays of equipment, history, etc.

Military Museums

Cabinet War Rooms
Clive Steps
King Charles Street
London SW1A 2AQ
Tel: 01-930 6961
Opening times: Tuesdays to Sundays and some Bank Holiday
Mondays 10.00am-5.50pm; closed some Bank Holidays and also
sometimes at short notice on State occasions
Admission: children £1.00, adults £2.00
Buses: 3, 11, 12, 24, 29, 53, 70, 77, 77A, 88, 109, 170, 184
BR station: Charing Cross
Underground: Westminster
Underground accommodation for War Cabinet, Chiefs of Staff,
Intelligence and Planning Staff and Prime Minister during
Second World War. Quiz sheets.
See walk 2.

HMS Belfast
Symons Wharf
Vine Lane
Tooley Street
London SE1 2JH
Tel: 01-407 6434
Opening times: 20 March to 31 October: daily 11.00am-
5.50pm; 1 November to 19 March: 11.00am-4.30pm; last
admission 30 minutes before closing time; closed some Bank
Holidays
Admission: children £1.00, adults £2.00
Buses: 10, 42, 44, 47, 48, 70, 78
BR station: London Bridge
Underground: London Bridge
Second World War cruiser in active service until 1963, and the
last survivor of the Royal Navy's big ships. Quiz sheets.
See walk 6.

Imperial War Museum
Lambeth Road
London SE1 6HZ
Tel: 01-735 8922
Opening times: Mondays to Saturdays 10.00am-5.50pm;
Sundays 2.00-5.50pm; closed some Bank Holidays
Admission: free
Buses: 3, 12, 44, 53, 109, 155, 159, 172, 184, 188
BR stations: Elephant and Castle, Waterloo
Underground: Elephant and Castle, Lambeth North
All aspects of the First and Second World Wars and other
conflicts since 1914 involving Britain and the Commonwealth.

Displays include tanks, aircraft, artillery, uniforms, photographs, documents, medals, paintings and posters. Regular special exhibitions. Worksheets and quiz sheets.

National Army Museum
Royal Hospital Road
London SW3 4HT
Tel: 01-730 0717
Opening times: Mondays to Saturdays 10.00am-5.30pm; Sundays 2.00-5.30pm; closed 1 January, Good Friday, May Day Holiday, 24-26 December
Admission: free
Buses: 11, 19, 22, 39, 137
BR station: Victoria
Underground: Sloane Square
History of the British Army from 1485 and of the Indian Army until 1947. Full programme of holiday events. Worksheets.

Royal Air Force Museum, Battle of Britain Museum and Bomber Command Museum
Grahame Park Way
Hendon
London NW9 5LL
Tel: 01-205 2266
Opening times: Mondays to Saturdays 10.00am-6.00pm; Sundays 2.00-6.00pm; closed 1 January, Good Friday, May Day Holiday, 24-26 December
Admission: free to RAF Museum; Battle of Britain and Bomber Command Museum children 50p each, adults £1.00 each
Bus: 79
BR station: Mill Hill Broadway, then 25 minute walk
Underground: Colindale
The RAF Museum contains a unique collection of over 40 aircraft. The Battle of Britain Museum re-creates the 1940 struggle between the RAF and the Luftwaffe, and the Bomber Aircraft Museum has a striking display of famous bomber aircraft. Trails and questionnaires.

Royal Hospital, Chelsea
Royal Hospital Road
Chelsea
London SW3 4SR
Tel: 01-730 0161
Opening times: Mondays to Saturdays 10.00am-12.00pm, 2.00-4.00pm; Sundays 2.00-4.00pm; closed Sundays from October to March and throughout Bank Holiday weekends.
Admission: free
Buses: 11, 39, 137
BR station: Victoria

Underground: Sloane Square
Great Hall, Chapel, and Museum of the hospital's history, which
has cared for veteran soldiers since the late 17th century.

Museums of Natural History

Horniman Museum & Library
London Road
Forest Hill
London SE23 3PQ
Tel: 01-699 2399; 01-699 1872; 01-699 4911
Opening times: Mondays to Saturdays 10.30 am-6.00 pm;
Sundays 2.00-6.00 pm
Admission: free
Buses: 12, 12A, 63, 122, 124, 171, 185, 194, P4
BR station: Forest Hill
Extensive ethnographic, natural history and musical instrument
collections. World-wide range of animals, displays illustrating
aspects of animal life. Live animal section including tropical
marine fish, reptiles and observation beehive.

Natural History Museum
Cromwell Road
London SW7 5BD
Tel: 01-589 6323
Opening times: Mondays to Saturdays 10.00 am-6.00 pm;
Sundays 2.30-6.00 pm; closed some Bank Holidays
Admission: free
Buses: 9, 14, 30, 33, 45, 49, 52, 52A, 73, 74
BR station: Victoria
Underground: South Kensington
Up-to-date exhibitions on dinosaurs, whales, ecology, evolution
and the human body, all designed to interest children. National
collections of fossils, rocks, minerals, birds, mammals, insects and
plants. Family Centre, with special hands-on activities at Easter
and during August. Worksheets.

Nature Reserve and Interpretative Centre
St Mary's Churchyard
Norman Road
East Ham
London E6
Tel: 01-470 4525
Opening times: Interpretative Centre: Tuesdays, Thursdays,
Saturdays and Sundays 2.00-5.00 pm

Nature reserve: daily 9.00 am-5.00 pm
Admission: free
Buses: 101, S1
BR stations: Manor Park, Woodgrange Park
Underground: East Ham
Exhibition of webs of life and food chains; nature trail through
4-hectare (9-acre) urban nature reserve maintained for
preservation of small animals, insects and birds.

Passmore Edwards Museum
Romford Road
Stratford
London E15 4LZ
Tel: 01-519 4296
Opening times: Mondays to Fridays 10.00 am-6.00 pm;
Saturdays 10.00 am-1.00 pm and 2.00-5.00 pm; Sundays and
Bank Holidays 2.00-5.00 pm
Admission: free
Buses: 25, 86, 225
BR station: Stratford
Underground: Stratford
Local natural history, and geology, history and archaeology of
geographical county of Essex (which includes north-east London).
Competition sheets during school holidays.

Royal Museums

Banqueting House
Whitehall
London SW1
Tel: 01-930 4179
Opening times: Tuesdays to Saturdays 10.00 am-5.00 pm;
Sundays 2.00-5.00 pm; may be closed at short notice for
government functions
Admission: children 25p, adults 50p
Buses: 3, 11, 12, 24, 29, 53, 77, 88, 159
BR station: Charing Cross
Underground: Charing Cross, Embankment, Westminster
Chief remaining part of the royal Palace of Whitehall, designed by
Inigo Jones.
See walk 1.

Eltham Palace
Eltham
London SE9

Tel: 01-859 2112 extension 255
Opening times: Thursdays and Sundays 10.30 am-12.15 pm,
2.15-6.00 pm or dusk, whichever is earlier
Admission: free
Buses: 21, 21A, 61, 108, 124, 124A, 126, 132, 160, 161, 228
BR stations: Eltham, Mottingham
Tudor royal palace with Great Hall and stone bridge across the
moat.

Hampton Court Palace

East Molesey
Surrey KT8 9AU
Tel: 01-977 8441
Opening times: 1 April to 30 September: Mondays to Saturdays
9.30 am-6.00 pm, Sundays 11.00 am-6.00 pm; 1 October to
31 March: Mondays to Saturdays 9.30 am-5.00 pm, Sundays
2.00-6.00 pm
Admission: children £1.00, adults £2.00
Buses: 111, 131, 216, 267, 461, 715, 716, 718, 726, 728
BR station: Hampton Court
As well as the state apartments, there is the Mantegna Paintings
Gallery, and the Great Kitchens and Cellars, Tudor Tennis
Court, King's Private Apartments and Hampton Court Exhibition
(all open April to September only). The gardens are all open to the
public daily until 9.00 pm or dusk, whichever is earlier. The maze
is open from March to October.

Imperial Collection

Central Hall
Westminster
London SW1
Tel: 01-222 0770
Opening times: April to October: daily 10.00 am-6.00 pm;
November to March: daily 11.00 am-6.00 pm
Admission: children £1.00, adults £2.00
Buses: 3, 11, 12, 24, 29, 53, 70, 76, 77, 77A, 88, 109, 159, 170,
184
BR stations: Charing Cross, Victoria
Underground: St James's Park, Westminster
Facsimiles of over 180 pieces of royal regalia, orbs, sceptres and
diamonds from more than 15 countries. Each piece has been
assembled by hand, and many of the pieces shown are the only
copies in existence, as the originals have been destroyed.
See walk 2.

Kensington Palace and the Court Collection

The Broad Walk
Kensington Gardens
London W8

Tel: 01-937 9561
Opening times: Mondays to Saturdays 9.00 am-5.00 pm;
Sundays 1.00-5.00 pm; closed some Bank Holidays; last tickets
sold 45 minutes before closing time
Buses: 9, 12, 33, 49, 52, 52A, 73, 88
Underground: High Street Kensington, Notting Hill,
Queensway
See walk 30.

Kew Palace and Queen's Cottage, Kew
Kew Gardens
Richmond
Surrey
Tel: 01-977 8441
Opening times: Palace: April to September: daily 11.00 am-
5.30 pm
Cottage: April to September: Saturdays, Sundays and Bank
Holidays 11.00 am-5.30 pm
Admission: Palace: children 30p, adults 60p
Cottage: children 15p, adults 30p
Buses: 15, 27, 65, 90B, 237, 267
BR stations: Kew Bridge, Kew Gardens
Underground: Kew Gardens

Royal Mews
Buckingham Palace
London SW1W 0QH
Tel: 01-930 4832 extension 634
Opening times: Wednesdays and Thursdays 2.00-4.00 pm; may
be closed on state occasions
Admission: children 15p, adults 30p
Buses: 2, 2B, 10, 11, 16, 24, 25, 29, 36, 36A, 36B, 38, 39, 52,
52A, 55, 70, 76, 149, 185, 500, 507
BR station: Victoria
Underground: St James's Park, Victoria
The Queen's carriages and horses.
See walk 1.

Museums of Science and Technology

Geological Museum
Exhibition Road
London SW7 2DE
Tel: 01-589 3444
Opening times: Mondays to Saturdays 10.00 am-6.00 pm;

Sundays 2.30-6.00pm; closed Bank Holidays
Admission: free
Buses: 9, 14, 30, 33, 45, 49, 52, 52A, 73, 74
BR station: Victoria
Underground: South Kensington
Every aspect of earth sciences, including 'The Story of Earth',
'Britain before Man', 'British Fossils', gems, the regional geology
and scenery of Great Britain, and minerals world-wide. A piece of
the Moon is also displayed. Worksheets.

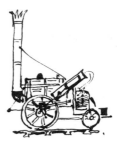

Kew Bridge Engines Trust
Green Dragon Lane
Brentford
Middlesex
Tel: 01-568 4757
Opening times: Sundays and Bank Holiday Mondays 11.00am-
5.00pm
Admission: children 80p, adults £1.40
Buses: 7, 27, 65, 237, 267
BR station: Kew Bridge
Underground: Gunnersbury
Five giant Cornish steam pumping engines, used to pump
London's water supply. A museum of London's water supply is
being created. The engines work in steam every weekend.

Science Museum
Exhibition Road
London SW7
Tel: 01-589 3456
Opening times: Mondays to Saturdays 10.00am-6.00pm;
Sundays 2.30-6.00pm; closed some Bank Holidays
Admission: free
Buses: 9, 14, 30, 33, 45, 49, 52, 52A, 73, 74
BR station: Victoria
Underground: South Kensington
London's most comprehensive museum of science, with
comprehensive (and often high-level) displays on every aspect of
hard science, and also medicine, computers, domestic science;
there is also a children's gallery. Worksheets and quizes.

Telecom Technology Showcase
135 Queen Victoria Street
London EC4V 4AT
Tel: 01-248 7444
Opening times: Mondays to Fridays 10.00am-5.00pm; closed
Bank Holidays
Admission: free
Buses: 45, 63, 76, 109, 141, 184
BR station: Blackfriars

Underground: Blackfriars
History and current development of the British telephone system.
See walk 8.

Muscums of Sport

Cricket Memorial Gallery

Lord's Ground
London NW8 8QN
Tel: 01-289 1611
Opening times: on match days, Mondays to Saturdays 10.30 am-
5.00 pm; on other days by prior appointment only (telephone
24 hours in advance)
Admission: children 25p, adults 50p
Buses: 2, 2B, 13, 16, 74, 74B, 113, 159
BR station: Marylebone
Underground: St John's Wood
History of cricket, with paintings, photographs, equipment,
memorabilia, and the Ashes.
See walk 9.

Wembley Stadium

Wembley
London HA9 0DW
Tel: 01-903 4864

Opening times: tours daily (except Thursdays) at 10.00 and
11.00 am, and at 12.00, 2.00, 3.00 and (in summer only) 4.00 pm;
closed during events at the Stadium, on the day before and on the
day after an event, and on New Year's Day
Admission: children £1.00, adults £1.80
Buses: 92, 182, 297
BR stations: Wembley Central, Wembley Complex
Underground: Wembley Park
Comprehensive guided tour round the stadium, including players'
changing rooms, players' tunnel, Royal Box, Wembley Trophy
Cabinet and audio-visual presentation.

Wimbledon Lawn Tennis Museum

The All England Club
Church Road
Wimbledon
London SW19
Tel: 01-946 6131

Opening times: Tuesdays to Saturdays 11.00 am-5.00 pm;
Sundays 2.00-5.00 pm; closed Bank Holidays and the Friday,

Saturday and Sunday prior to the annual Championships and the
Sundays during and after them
Admission: children 75p, adults £1.50
Underground: Southfields
The Wimbledon Championships, and the history and
development of the game of lawn tennis. Fashion, trophies,
equipment and audio-visual display. The Centre Court can also
be viewed.

Museums of Toys and Social Life

Bethnal Green Museum of Childhood
Cambridge Heath Road
London ER2 9PA
Tel: 01-980 2415
Opening times: Mondays to Thursdays and Saturdays 10.00 am-
6.00 pm; Sundays 2.00-6.00 pm; closed some Bank Holidays
Admission: free
Buses: 6, 6A, 8, 8A, 35, 106, 253
BR station: Cambridge Heath Road
Underground: Bethnal Green
Toys – including wooden toys, metal toys such as toy soldiers,
clockwork railways, teddy bears and other soft toys, board games –
dolls, dolls' houses, puppets, and childrens' dress. Worksheets
sometimes available.

Geffrye Museum of Furniture
and Decorative Arts
Kingsland Road
Shoreditch
London E2 8EA
Tel: 01-739 9893; 01-739 8368
Opening times: Tuesdays to Sundays and Bank Holidays
10.00 am-5.00 pm; Sundays 2.00-5.00 pm
Admission: free
Buses: 22, 22A, 48, 67, 149, 243
BR station: Liverpool Street
Underground: Liverpool Street, Old Street
Furniture in period room settings. Puzzle sheets and Saturday
holiday workshops.

Gunnersbury Park Museum
Gunnersbury Park
London W3 8LQ
Tel: 01-992 1612
Opening times: March to October: Mondays to Fridays 1.00-
5.00 pm; Saturdays, Sundays and Bank Holidays 2.00-6.00 pm;

November to February: Mondays to Fridays 1.00-5.00pm;
Saturdays, Sundays and Bank Holidays 2.00-4.00pm
Admission: free
Buses: 7, E3
BR station: Gunnersbury
Underground: Acton Central
Local history collection includes costume, toys and dolls.

Linley Sambourne House
18 Stafford Terrace
Kensington
London W8
Tel: 01-994 1019 (Victorian Society)
Opening times: 1 March to 31 October: Wednesdays 10.00 am-
4.00pm; Sundays 2.00-5.00pm
Admission: children 75p, adults £1.50
Buses: 9, 27, 28, 31, 33, 49, 73
BR station: Paddington
Underground: High Street Kensington
Unique survival of a late-Victorian house with its original
furnishings and decorations, providing a fascinating record of how
people lived 100 years ago.

London Toy and Model Museum
21/23 Craven Hill
London W2 3EN
Tel: 01-262 7905; 01-262 9450; 01-262 9350
Opening times: Tuesdays to Saturdays and Bank Holiday
Mondays 10.00 am-5.30pm; Sundays 11.00 am-5.00 pm
Admission: children 60p, adults £1.80
Buses: 12, 88
BR station: Paddington
Underground: Lancaster Gate, Paddington
Commercially manufactured toys from the Industrial Revolution,
with the emphasis on mechanical toys: trains and boats, including
live steam trains, ride-on steam train and carousel. Dolls, bears,
etc. Boating pond. Quiz sheets.

Pollock's Toy Museum
1 Scala Street
London W1P 1LT
Tel: 01-636 3452
Opening times: Mondays to Saturdays 10.00 am-5.00 pm; closed
Bank Holidays
Admission: children 20p, adults 50p
Buses: 14, 24, 29, 73, 134, 176
BR station: Euston
Underground: Goodge Street

Fascinating toy museum, with space and optical toys, puppets, wax and composition dolls, toy soldiers, dolls' houses, china, wood, rag and celluloid dolls and the toy theatre, from Britain and abroad.

Victoria and Albert Museum

South Kensington
London SW7
Tel: 01-589 6371
Opening times: Mondays to Thursdays and Saturdays 10.00 am-5.50 pm; Sundays 2.30-5.50 pm; closed Fridays and some Bank Holidays
Admission: free
Buses: 14, 30, 45, 49
BR station: Victoria
Underground: South Kensington
Comprehensive collection on the fine and applied arts from the 16th to the 20th centuries.

Transport Museums

CS Cutty Sark

King William Walk
Greenwich
London SE10
Tel: 01-858 3445
Opening times: summer: Mondays to Saturdays 10.30 am-6.00 pm; Sundays 12.00-6.00 pm; winter: Mondays to Saturdays 10.30 am-5.00 pm; Sundays 12.00-5.00 pm
Admission: children 50p, adults £1.00
Buses: 177, 180, 185, 188
BR station: Greenwich
See walk 12.

Gipsy Moth IV

c/o CS Cutty Sark
King William Walk
Greenwich
London SE10
Tel: 01-858 3445
Opening times: summer: Mondays to Saturdays 10.30 am-6.00 pm; Sundays 12.00-6.00 pm; closed in winter
Admission: children 10p, adults 20p
Buses: 170, 180, 185, 188
BR station: Greenwich
See walk 12.

Gunnersbury Park Museum
Gunnersbury Park
London W3 8LQ
Tel: 01-992 1612
Opening times: March to October: Mondays to Fridays 1.00-
5.00pm; Saturdays, Sundays and Bank Holidays 2.00-4.00pm
Admission: free
Buses: 7, E3
BR station: Gunnersbury
Underground: Acton Town
Local history collection; includes material on transport.

Heritage Motor Museum
Syon Park
Brentford
Middlesex TW8 8JF
Tel: 01-560 1378
Opening times: March to October: daily 10.00am-5.30pm;
November to February: daily 10.00am-4.00pm
Admission: children 90p, adults £1.60, family £3.75
Buses: 237, 267
BR stations: Brentford Central, Syon Lane
Large collection of historic British cars. Production cars from
1895 to present day, prototypes, rallying, racing and record-
breaking cars.

Historic Ship Collection
Maritime Trust
52 St Katharine's Way
London E1 9LB
Tel: 01-481 0043
Opening times: April to October: daily 10.00am-6.00pm;
November to March: daily 10.00am-5.00pm
Admission: children 80p, adults £1.60
Buses: 23, 42, 56, 78
BR station: Fenchurch Street
Underground: Tower Hill
Seven historic working vessels, including Captain Scott's
Discovery.
See walk 6.

London Transport Museum
Covent Garden
London WC2E 7BB
Tel: 01-379 6344
Opening times: daily 10.00am-6.00pm; last admission 5.15pm
Admission: children £1.00, adults £2.20
Buses: 1, 1A, 4, 5, 6, 9, 11, 13, 15, 23, 68, 77, 77A, 155, 170,

171, 176, 188, 501, 502, 513
BR station: Charing Cross
Underground: Covent Garden
Complete collection of London Transport vehicles and
locomotives: horsebuses, motorbuses, trams, trolleybuses and
Underground trains. Unique working exhibits – you can 'drive' a
bus, a tram and a tube train.
See walk 4.

National Maritime Museum and Old Royal Observatory
Greenwich
London SE10 9NF
Tel: 01-858 4422
Opening times: summer: Mondays to Saturdays 10.00 am-
6.00 pm; Sundays 2.00-5.30 pm; winter: Mondays to Fridays
10.00 am-5.00 pm; Saturdays 10.00 am-5.30 pm; Sundays 2.00-
5.00 pm; closed some Bank Holidays
Admission: children 75p, adults £1.50
Buses: 108B, 177, 180, 185, 188
BR stations: Greenwich, Maze Hill
See walk 12.

North Woolwich Old Station Museum
Pier Road
London E16 2JJ
Tel: 01-474 7244
Opening times: Mondays to Saturdays 10.00 am-5.00 pm;
Sundays and Bank Holidays 2.00-5.00 pm
Admission: free
Buses: 58, 69, 101
BR station: North Woolwich
History of the Great Eastern Railway with operating steam
locomotives. Competition sheets during school holidays.

Science Museum
Exhibition Road
London SW7
Tel: 01-589 3456
Opening times: Mondays to Saturdays 10.00 am-6.00 pm;
Sundays 2.30-6.00 pm; closed some Bank Holidays
Admission: free
Buses: 9, 14, 30, 33, 45, 49, 52, 52A, 73, 74
BR station: Victoria
Underground: South Kensington
Includes galleries on railway and aircraft history.

Southall Railway Centre
Merrick Road
Southall
Middlesex
Tel: 01-574 1529
Opening times: Saturdays and Sundays 11.00 am-6.00 pm
Admission: steaming days: children 60p, adults £1.20; other
days: children 30p, adults 60p
Buses: 89, 105, 120, 195, 232
BR station: Southall
Great Western Railway preservation group.

Thames Barrier Visitors Centre
Unity Way
Woolwich
London SE18 5NJ
Tel: 01-854 1375
Opening times: 1 April to 30 September: daily 10.30 am-
6.00 pm; 1 October to 31 March: daily 10.30 am-5.00 pm
Admission: free
Buses: 51, 96, 161, 177, 180 and shuttle service from Greenwich
in the summer
BR station: Charlton
Four river sailings a day from Westminster Pier to the Barrier
Gardens Pier. Tel.: 01-930 3373 for further information.
Exhibition centre explaining why the Barrier, a unique flood
defence system that protects central London, is necessary, and the
history of its construction; models and photographs; large working
sectional model; electronically controlled multi-media show and
video presentation. Boat trip through the Barrier gates.

Vestry House Museum
Vestry Road
Walthamstow
London E17 9NH
Tel: 01-527 5544 extension 4391
Opening times: Mondays to Fridays 10.00 am-5.30 pm;
Saturdays 10.00 am-5.00 pm; closed between 1.00 and 2.00 pm
Wednesdays and Saturdays; closed Bank Holidays
Admission: free
Buses: 69, 97, 97A, 212, 275
BR station: Walthamstow Central
Underground: Walthamstow Central
This museum of local history also contains the Bremer car,
reputedly the first British-built four-wheeled internal combustion
engine.

189

Outdoor London
Parks, outside central London

Bayhurst Wood
Entrance: Breakspear Road North, Ruislip
Buses: 114, 128, E2
BR station: West Ruislip
Underground: West Ruislip, Ruislip
Country park (40 hectares/98 acres) with walks, nature trails and picnic facilities.

Burgess Park
Albany Road
London SE5
Tel: 01-703 3911
Buses: 12, 35, 40, 42, 45, 68, 171, 176, 184, P3
BR station: Elephant and Castle
Underground: Elephant and Castle
A new park still being developed in a densely populated area. Sports facilities, adventure playground, paddling pool, fishing lake, information centre.

Bushey Park
Buses: 111, 216, 267, 718, 726
BR stations: Hampton, Hampton Court
Attractive park bordering on the Thames west of Hampton Court Palace, beyond the formal gardens of the palace.

Crystal Palace Park
Anerley Road
London SE19
Tel: 01-778 7148
Buses: 2B, 3, 63, 108B, 122, 137, 157, 227, 249
BR station: Crystal Palace
Large park with children's zoo, adventure playground and boating lake in the grounds of the now-destroyed Crystal Palace. The Victorian dinosaurs along the lakeside are a perennial fascination for children. There is also a concert bowl where Sunday-evening concerts are given in July and August. The National Sports Centre is also in the park.

Dulwich Park
College Road
Dulwich Village
London SE19
Tel: 01-693 5737
Buses: 3, 37, 12, 63, P4

BR stations: North Dulwich, West Dulwich
An old-established park near attractive Dulwich Village, with
bowling and putting greens, boating lake, aviary and tree trail.
Excellent display of flowers, especially rhododendrons and
azaleas.

Park Wood

Entrance: Bury Street, Ruislip
Buses: 114, E2
BR station: West Ruislip
Underground: Ruislip
An area of woodland (96 hectares/238 acres) adjoining Ruislip
Lido and once part of Forest of Middlesex. 3-kilometre (2-mile)
nature trail.

Richmond Park

Buses: 71
BR station: Richmond
Underground: Richmond
East of Richmond, between Richmond and Roehampton. Royal
park with 1,000 hectares (2,500 acres) of woodland and common
land with magnificent trees, shrubs and woodland; much wildlife
including red and fallow deer.

Royal Botanic Gardens

Kew
Richmond
Surrey TW9 3AB
Tel: 01-940 1171
Opening times: Park: 10.00am-dusk or 8.00pm, whichever is
earlier.
Museums: Mondays to Saturdays 10.00am-4.50pm; Sundays
10.00am-5.50pm.
Glasshouses: Mondays to Saturdays 11.00am-4.50pm; Sundays
11.00am-5.50pm (earlier in winter)
Admission: children under 10 free, adults 15p
Buses: 7, 27, 65
BR stations: Kew Bridge, Kew Gardens
Underground: Kew Gardens
Landscaped gardens (120 hectares/300 acres) with over 50,000
different types of plant from all over the world. Glasshouses,
pagoda, orangery, museums. Ferns, orchids and many rare
specimens. Trees, shrubs, alpine plants, herbaceous plants.

Other large parks and open spaces worth visiting are:

Alexandra Park and the Palace
Bedford Park
Eltham Park

Epping Forest
Greenwich Park (see walk 14)
Hainault Forest
Hampstead Heath (see walk 15)
Osterley Park, Hounslow
Trent Park, Enfield
Victoria Park
Wanstead Flats
Wimbledon Common

Urban walks

Green Chain Walk
Start: Thamesmead
Buses: 198, 198A, 272
BR station: Abbey Wood
or
Start: Thames Barrier,
Unity Way, Woolwich
Buses: 177, 180
BR station: Charlton

Finish: Cator Park, Beckenham
Bus: 227
BR station: Kent House
This is a 25-kilometre (15½-mile) waymarked walk from the
Thames at the Thames Barrier and further east at Thamesmead
through south-east London to Kent House, near Beckenham. It
passes through a string of 300 public and private open spaces,
including woodlands, parks, gardens, grasslands. There are good
views, and the walk runs past such historic sites as Eltham Palace,
whose surviving Great Hall was built in 1475, and the ruined
monastery in Lesnes Abbey Woods.

Parkland Walk
Start: Oxford Road, Finsbury Park
Buses: 210, W2, W3, W7
BR station: Finsbury Park
Underground: Finsbury Park

Finish: Muswell Hill, at entrance to Alexandra Palace and Park
Buses: 144, 144A, W7, W9
BR station: Alexandra Park
Underground: Highgate
Walk along railway line that used to connect Finsbury Park station
and Alexandra Palace, running through Queens and Highgate
Woods. About 6 kilometres (3¾ miles).

Spitalfields Walk
Start and finish: Brushfield Street, on the corner of Bishopsgate
Buses: 5, 6, 8, 8A, 22, 22A, 35, 47, 48, 78, 149, 243A
Underground: Liverpool Street
Around the centre of London's once-flourishing silk industry, where the Jack the Ripper murders took place, and now a hotchpotch of nationalities and trades.

Thames-side
Start: Richmond
Buses: 7, 27
BR station: Richmond
Underground: Richmond

Finish: Kingston
Buses: 5, 7, 85, 213, 246, 406, 476, 478, 479, 713
BR station: Kingston
Lovely walk along Thames from Richmond through Petersham Meadows and Ham Fields to Kingston.

Walworth Walk
Buses: 12, 35, 42, 45, 53, 63, 68, 171, 184, 188
BR station: Elephant and Castle
Underground: Elephant and Castle
Walk through Walworth, a contrasting area of early to late Victorian housing and modern high- and low-rise estates; runs through colourful East Street Market.
Leaflet obtainable from London Borough of Southwark Planning Department, (Planning Division), 30-32 Peckham Road, London SE5 8QP.

Whitechapel Walk
Start: Aldgate East Underground Station
Buses: 5, 10, 15, 15A, 22A, 25, 40, 67, 225, 253
Underground: Aldgate East
Around a fascinating part of the East End, settled by Jews and more recently by Bengalis, with the street market on Whitechapel Road. Leaflet from Tower Hamlets Tourist Information Office, 88 Roman Road, E2. Tel: 01-980 3749

Puppetry and Puppet Theatres

Little Angel Marionette Theatre
14 Dagmar Passage
Cross Street
London N1 2DN
Tel: 01-226 1767

Admission: children £1.00-£1.75, adults £2.00-£2.75
Buses: 4, 19, 30, 38, 43, 73, 104, 171, 277, 279
BR station: Essex Road
Underground: Angel, Highbury & Islington
Wide variety of puppetry performances of all types, including
visiting companies from abroad.

Polka Children's Theatre
240 The Broadway
Wimbledon
London SW19 1SB
Tel: 01-543 4888 (box office); 01-542 4258 (administration)
Admission: children £1.20-£2.90, adults £2.00-£5.80
Buses: 57, 93, 155, 293
BR station: Wimbledon
Underground: South Wimbledon, Wimbledon
Celebrated children's theatre that includes puppet shows in its
repertoire, sometimes with Ultra-Violet-lit puppets or a Shadow
Puppet show in the Far East tradition; puppet workshops also
held.

Watermans Arts Centre
40 High Street
Brentford
Middlesex
Tel: 01-568 3312
Buses: 65, 27, 237, 267
BR stations: Brentford, Kew Bridge
Underground: Gunnersbury
Regular weekend clown and puppet shows.

Recreation Centres

Britannia Leisure Centre
Hyde Road
London N1
Tel: 01-729 4485
Buses: 5, 22, 22A, 35, 48, 55, 67, 76, 141, 149, 243, 271
BR station: Old Street
Underground: Old Street
Aerobics, badminton, basketball, football, gymnastics, judo and
martial arts, keep fit, netball, solarium, squash, swimming, tennis,
volleyball, weight training.

Brixton Recreation Centre
Brixton Station Road
London SW9
Tel: 01-274 7774
Buses: 2, 2B, 3, 35, 37, 45, 50, 59, 95, 109, 133, 159, 172, 189, 196
BR station: Brixton
Underground: Brixton
Archery, bowls, climbing, cricket, golf, gymnastics, rifle-shooting, sauna and solarium, squash, street hockey, swimming, table tennis, weight training. Dance, theatre, music.

Bromley Civic Centre Sports Hall
Rochester Avenue
Bromley BR1 3UH
Tel: 01-464 3333 extension 5445
Buses: 227
BR stations: Bromley North, Bromley South
Badminton, basketball, keep fit, martial arts, netball, trampolining, volleyball.

Crofton Leisure Centre
Manwood Road
Crofton Park
Brockley
London SE4 1SA
Tel: 01-690 0273
Buses: 36A, 86, 122, 141, 171
BR station: Crofton Park
Aerobics, badminton, dance, gymnastics, judo, karate, keep fit and circuit training, table tennis, trampoline, volleyball.

Durnsford Recreation Centre
Rhodes Avenue
London N22
Tel: 01-881 3610
Buses: 102, W9
BR station: Alexandra Park
Underground: Bounds Green
Aerobics, badminton, basketball, cricket nets, 5-a-side football, karate, keep fit, netball, popmobility, short tennis, table tennis, trampolining, volleyball. Drama hall and two music rooms.

Eastway Sports Centre
Quarter Mile Lane
Leyton
London E10
Tel: 01-519 0017
Buses: 6, 30, 236
BR station: Stratford
Underground: Leyton
Badminton, basketball, cricket, 5-a-side football, football,
gymnastics, hockey, keep fit, netball, rugby, squash, tennis,
trampolining, volleyball.

Elephant & Castle Recreation Centre
22 Elephant and Castle
London SE1
Tel: 01-582 5505
Buses: 1, 1A, 10, 12, 44, 45, 53, 63, 68, 109, 141, 155, 171, 176,
177, 184, 188
BR station: Elephant and Castle
Underground: Elephant and Castle
Badminton, basketball, cricket nets, 5-a-side soccer, netball,
sauna, squash, swimming, table tennis, trampolining, volleyball.
Regular classes.

Finsbury Leisure Centre
Norman Street
London EC1
Tel: 01-253 2346
Buses: 4, 5, 55, 243, 277, 279A
BR station: Old Street
Underground: Old Street
Badminton, dance, 5-a-side football, netball, roller-skating rink,
sports hall, squash courts, tennis, weight training.

George Sylvester Sports Centre
Wilton Way
London E8
Tel: 01-985 2105
Buses: 22, 22A, 38, 96, 277
BR station: Hackney Downs, Hackney Central, London Fields
Aerobics, gymnastics, judo, karate, keep fit, rifle range, solarium.

Harlington Sports Centre
Harlington Upper School
Pinkwell Lane
Harlington
Middlesex
Tel: 01-848 0839

Buses: 90B, 98, 140
BR station: Hayes
Archery, badminton, basketball, cricket, gymnastics, handball,
hockey, judo, karate, keep-fit, netball, sauna, soccer, table tennis,
tennis, trampolining, volleyball, weight-training room.

Harrow Leisure Centre

Christchurch Avenue
Harrow
Middlesex
Tel: 01-863 5611 extension 2724; 01-863 9580 (bookings)
Buses: H1
BR station: Harrow & Wealdstone
Underground: Kenton
Badminton, basketball, bowls, cricket nets, 5-a-side football,
hockey, netball, sauna, snooker, squash, swimming, table tennis,
tennis, volleyball, weight training.

Hayes Manor Sports Centre

Hayes Manor School
Wood End Green Road
Hayes End
Middlesex
Tel: 01-561 8448
Buses: 204, 207
Underground: Uxbridge
Archery, badminton, basketball, cricket, gymnastics, handball,
hockey, judo, karate, keep fit, modern dance, netball, soccer, table
tennis, tennis, trampolining, volleyball, yoga.

John Penrose Sports Centre

Northwood Way
Harefield
Middlesex
Tel: Harefield (089 582) 2929
Buses: 128, 348, 378
Archery, badminton, basketball, gymnastics, keep fit, martial arts,
netball, popmobility, table tennis, trampolining, volleyball.

Jubilee Sports Centre

Caird Street
Paddington
London W10
Tel: 01-798 3580
Buses: 18
BR station: Queens Park
Underground: Westbourne Park
Badminton, basketball, cricket, 5-a-side football, gymnastics, keep
fit, martial arts, netball, swimming, table tennis, tennis,
trampolining, volleyball, weight training.

The Langham Sports Centre

Langham Road
London N15
Tel: 01-889 5111
Buses: 41, 67, 171
BR station: Seven Sisters
Underground: Seven Sisters, Turnpike Lane
Badminton, basketball, cricket nets, 5-a-side football, martial arts,
netball, short tennis, squash, table tennis, volleyball.

Lewisham Leisure Centre and Riverdale Hall

Rennel Street
Lewisham
London SE13 7EP
Tel: 01-318 4421
Buses: 1, 21, 36, 36B, 47, 54, 84, 94, 108B, 122, 151, 180, 185,
192
BR station: Lewisham
Archery, badminton, bowls, cricket, cricket nets, golf, gymnastics,
judo, karate, keep fit, martial arts, netball, shooting, table tennis,
trampolining, volleyball, yoga.

Michael Sobell Sports Centre

Hornsey Road
London N7
Tel: 01-607 1632
Buses: 14
BR station: Drayton Park
Underground: Holloway Road Arsenal
Badminton, climbing wall, cricket, ice rink, sauna, snooker, sports
hall, squash courts, weight training.

National Recreation Centre

Anerley Road
London SE19
Tel: 01-778 0131
Buses: 2B, 3, 63, 108B, 122, 137, 157, 227, 249
BR station: Crystal Palace
Badminton, diving, gymnastics, keep fit, netball, ski slope, squash,
swimming, tennis, volleyball, weight training.

New River Sports Centre

White Hart Lane
London N22
Tel: 01-881 1926
Buses: 29, 123, 221, 298, W3, W4
BR station: White Hart Lane

Underground: Wood Green
Athletics, badminton, basketball, cricket nets, football, hockey, jogging and trimtrail, netball, pitch and putt, rugby, tennis, weight lifting.

Northumberland Park Sports Centre
Worcester Avenue
Tottenham
London N17
Tel: 01-801 9364
Buses: 149, 259, 279, 279A
BR stations: Northumberland Park, White Hart Lane
Underground: Seven Sisters
All-weather pitch, basketball, cricket nets, multi-purpose sports hall, netball, swimming pool, tennis.

Northwood Sports Centre
Potter Street
Northwood
Middlesex
Tel: Northwood (092 74) 24833
Buses: 183, 282
Underground: Northwood Hills
Badminton, cricket, gymnastics, karate, popmobility, soccer, table tennis, tennis.

Picketts Lock Centre
Montague Road
Edmonton
London N9
Tel: 01-803 4756
Buses: 76, 149, 191, 238, 279, W8
BR station: Lower Edmonton
Badminton, bowls, 5-a-side football, football, golf, hockey, keep fit, netball, roller skating, sauna and solarium, snooker, squash, swimming, trampolining, volleyball, weight training.

Queen Elizabeth's Centre
Meadway
Barnet
Hertfordshire
Tel: 01-441 2933
Buses: 26
BR station: New Barnet
Underground: High Barnet
Badminton, basketball, contemporary and modern dance, cricket nets, football, gymnastics, netball, popmobility, swimming, table tennis, tennis, trampolining, volleyball, water polo, weight training, yoga.

Queen Mother Sports Centre
Vauxhall Bridge Road
Victoria
London SW1
Tel: 01-798 2125
Buses: 2, 2B, 36, 36A, 36B, 185
BR station: Victoria
Underground: Victoria
Badminton, boxing, diving, 5-a-side football, gymnastics, keep fit, martial arts, squash, swimming, table tennis, tennis, trampolining, volleyball, weight training.

Queensmead Sports Centre
Victoria Road
South Ruislip
Middlesex
Tel: 01-845 6010
Buses: 114
BR station: South Ruislip
Underground: South Ruislip
Badminton, basketball, handball, indoor hockey, judo, netball, volleyball.

Redbridge Sports Centre
Forest Road
Barkingside
Essex IG6 3HD
Tel: 01-501 0019/20
Buses: 150, 167, 169, 247, 275
BR station: Ilford
Underground: Fairlop
Badminton, judo, racketball, tennis, trampoline.

Seymour Leisure Centre
Bryanston Place
St Marylebone
London W1
Tel: 01-723 8018; 01-402 5065
Buses: 1, 2, 2B, 13, 18, 27, 30, 74, 113, 159, 176
BR station: Marylebone
Underground: Edgware Road, Marble Arch
Badminton, basketball, 5-a-side football, gymnastics, ladies gym, sauna, squash, swimming, table tennis, trampolining, weight training.

Shene Sports Centre
Hertford Avenue
London SW14
Tel: 01-878 7107
Buses: 33, 37
BR station: Mortlake
Athletics, badminton, basketball, cricket, football, hockey, indoor hockey, netball, table tennis, tennis, trampolining, volleyball.

Tottenham Sports Centre
701 High Road
Tottenham
London N17 88X
Tel: 01-801 6401
Buses: 149, 259, 279, 279A
BR station: White Hart Lane
Underground: Seven Sisters
Badminton, basketball, boxing, 5-a-side football, martial arts, netball, rifle-shooting, roller skating, snooker, table tennis, weight training.

Walnuts Sports Centre
Lych Gate Road
Orpington
Kent
Tel: Orpington (66) 70533
Buses: 51, 61, 208, 229, 261, 284, 477, 493
BR station: Orpington
Archery, badminton, basketball, bridge, chess, fencing, 5-a-side football, golf practice, gymnastics, hockey, judo, karate, keep fit, netball, sauna, snooker, squash, swimming, table tennis, trampolining, weight training.

Wanstead Leisure Centre
Wanstead High School
Redbridge Lane West
London E11
Tel: 01-989 1172/3
Buses: 10, 66, 101, 148, 162, 206, 235
BR station: Ilford
Underground: Redbridge, Wanstead
Aerobics, badminton, basketball, 5-a-side football, gymnastics, hockey, indoor cricket, judo, ju-jitsu, keep-fit, netball, running, squash, swimming, table tennis, tennis, trampoline.

Westcroft Sports and Leisure Centre

Westcroft Road
Carshalton
Surrey
Tel: 01-669 7026
Buses: 157, 234A, 403, 408
BR stations: Carshalton, Carshalton Beeches, Hackbridge,
Wallington
Aerobics, archery, badminton, basketball, circuit training, cricket,
disco and jazz dance, exercise and dance, fencing, 5-a-side
football, golf practice, gymnastics, health play, indoor hockey,
karate, keep fit, kendo, korfball, lacrosse, netball, popmobility,
racketball, self-defence, short tennis, swimming, table squash,
table tennis, tennis, trampolining, volleyball, yoga.

Theatres

Albany Empire

Douglas Way
Deptford
London E8
Tel: 01-691 8016
Membership: 50p for one night, £1.00 for 4 months, £2.50 for a
year
Buses: 1, 47, 53, 177
BR stations: Deptford, New Cross
Underground: New Cross
Performances on the last Saturday of each month.

Lauderdale Community Arts Centre

Lauderdale House
Waterlow Park
Highgate Hill
London N6 5HG
Tel: 01-348 8716
Buses: 210, 143, 271
Underground: Archway
Regular Saturday morning shows.

Lyric Theatre

King Street
Hammersmith
London W6
Tel: 01-741 2311 (box office); 01-741 0824 (administration)
Admission: £1.00 for Saturday shows
Buses: 27, 91, 267
Underground: Hammersmith
Children's shows most Saturdays at 11.00am followed by special
children's lunches.

Molecule Theatre of Science
Mermaid Theatre
Puddle Dock
Blackfriars
London EC4
Tel: 01-236 9521 extension 259
Admission: children 50p, adults £1.00
Buses: 45, 63, 76, 109, 141, 184
BR station: Blackfriars
Underground: Blackfriars, St Paul's
Scientific adventure plays for 4-11 year olds. Molecule
Discussions; occasional series of illustrated scientific lectures for
13-18 year olds given by eminent scientists.

National Theatre
South Bank
London SE1 9PX
Tel: 01-928 2083
Buses: 1, 4, 5, 68, 70, 76, 149, 168A, 171, 176, 188, 239, 501,
513
BR station: Waterloo
Underground: Waterloo
Workshops, story-telling, puppet shows, clowning, mainly at
Christmas and during the summer holidays.

Orange Tree Theatre
45 Kew Road
Richmond
Surrey
Tel: 01-940 3633
Admission: £1.00-£1.50 for children's shows
Buses: 65, 71, 90B, 202, 290
BR station: Richmond
Underground: Richmond
Regular production for 3-8 year olds during summer half-term at
the end of May.

Polka Children's Theatre
240 The Broadway
Wimbledon
London SW19 1SB
Tel: 01-543 4888 (box office); 01-542 4258 (administration)
Admission: children £1.20-£2.90, adults £2.00-£5.80
Buses: 57, 93, 155, 293
BR station: Wimbledon
Underground: South Wimbledon, Wimbledon
One of London's most celebrated children's theatres, staging
work exclusively for children. A wide variety of shows, mixing
mime, masks, magic, music, dance, straight drama and puppetry.
Visits behind the scenes also available.

203

Queen's Theatre
Billet Lane
Hornchurch
Essex RM11 1ET
Tel: 04024-43333 (box office); 04024-56118 (administration)
Admission: children £2.10-£2.40, adults £3.30-£4.80
Buses: 193, 226, 246, 248, 256, 294, 370, 371
BR stations: Emerson Park, Romford
Underground: Hornchurch
Occasional weeks' performances by visiting children's theatre companies.

Richmond Theatre
The Green
Richmond
Surrey
Tel: 01-940 0088
Buses: 27, 33, 37, 65, 71, 90B, 202, 290
BR station: Richmond
Underground: Richmond
Traditional Christmas pantomime, and some children's plays at other times of the year.

Riverside Studios
Crisp Road
Hammersmith
London W6 9RL
Tel: 01-748 3354 (box office); 01-741 2251 (administration)
Admission: 50p for children's Saturday shows; £3.00-£4.00 for other shows
Buses: 9, 9A, 11, 33, 73, 220, 266, 267, 290
Underground: Hammersmith
Regular children's shows every Saturday at 12.30pm for about 1 hour; family shows from time to time, e.g. at Christmas.

Royal Festival Hall
South Bank
London SE1 8XX
Tel: 01-928 3191 (box office); 01-928 3641 (administration)
Buses: 1, 68, 70, 76, 171, 176, 177, 188, 507
BR station: Waterloo
Underground: Waterloo
Concerts and other music and dance events for children at different times throughout the year.

Sadler's Wells Theatre
Rosebery Avenue
London EC1R 4TN

Tel: 01-278 6563
Buses: 19, 30, 38, 171
BR stations: King's Cross, St Pancras
Underground: Angel
Whirligig children's theatre during autumn; Christmas show;
specialist children's shows whenever possible.

St Georges Theatre
49 Tufnell Park Road
Islington
London N7 0PS
Tel: 01-617 1128
Admission: 80p for children's Saturday afternoon shows
Buses: 4, 19, 43, 104, 172, 271
BR station: King's Cross
Underground: Holloway Road, Tufnell Park
Saturday afternoon shows for children aged from 3 to 12.

Tricycle Theatre
269 Kilburn High Road
London NW6
Tel: 01-328 8628
Admission: children £1.00, adults £2.50-£4.50
Buses: 8, 16, 32, 176
BR station: Kilburn
Underground: Kilburn
Regular performances on Saturdays at 11.30 am and during half-
terms and school holidays.

Unicorn Theatre for Children
6-7 Great Newport Street
London WC2
Tel: 01-836 3334
Membership: temporary 10p, full £3.00
Admission: £2.50-£3.50
Buses: 1, 24, 29, 176
BR station: Charing Cross
Underground: Leicester Square
Regular productions for children of specific ages from 4 to 12
between September and May.

Watermans Arts Centre
40 High Street
Brentford
Middlesex
Tel: 01-568 3312
Admission: children £1.25, adults £3.80
Buses: 27, 65, 237, 267

BR stations: Brentford, Kew Bridge
Underground: Gunnersbury, South Ealing
Christmas and summer theatre shows; regular clown and puppet
shows at weekends.

Waxworks

Madame Tussaud's
Marylebone Road
London NW1 5LR
Tel: 01-935 6861
Opening times: daily 10.00am-5.30pm
Admission: children £1.85, adults £3.30; combined ticket with
Planetarium next door children £2.55, adults £4.45
Buses: 2, 13, 18, 27, 30, 113, 159, 176
BR stations: Euston, Marylebone, Paddington
Underground: Baker Street
About 350 wax figures, and historical tableaux, Chamber of
Horrors, Battle of Trafalgar.

Zoos and Nature Reserves

The Butterfly Centre
Theobalds Park Road
Crews Hill
Enfield
Middlesex EN2 9BD
Tel: 01-363 7288
Opening times: March to October: daily 10.00am-6.00pm;
November to February: daily 10.00am-4.00pm
Admission: children 70p, adults £1.15
BR station: Crews Hill
Tropical garden among free-flying butterflies. Pictorial and
educational displays. Eight tropical fish centres, and Whitewebbs
Park nature trail.

Chessington Zoo
Leatherhead Road
Chessington
Surrey KT9 2NE
Tel: Epsom (78) 27227
Opening times: daily 10.00am-5.00pm
Admission: children £1.85, adults £3.25
Buses: 65, 71, 468
BR station: Chessington South
Children's zoo, bird garden, reptile house and all the usual zoo
animals.

London Butterfly Centre

Syon House
Brentford
Middlesex
Tel: 01-560 7272
Opening times: British Summer Time: daily 10.00 am-5.00 pm;
British Standard Time: daily 10.00 am-3.00 pm
Admission: children £1.00, adults £1.80
Buses: 237, 267
BR stations: Brentford Central, Syon Lane
Vast free-flying collection of butterflies from all over the world.

London Zoo

Outer Circle
Regent's Park
London NW1 4RY
Tel: 01-722 3333
Opening times: 1 March to 31 October: Mondays to Saturdays
9.00 am-6.00 pm or dusk, whichever is earlier, Sundays and Bank
Holidays 9.00 am-7.00 pm; 1 November to 28 February: daily
10.00 am-dusk
Admission: £1.60 children, adults £3.20
Buses: 3, 53, 74
Underground: Camden Town
More than 8,000 animals: mammals, birds, reptiles, fish,
amphibians, insects, etc. Children's Zoo. Animal rides during the
summer and other activities such as elephant weigh-in, Meet the
Animals Show.

Nature Reserve and Interpretative Centre

St Mary's Churchyard
Norman Road
East Ham
London E6
Tel: 01-470 4525
Opening times: Interpretative Centre: Tuesdays, Thursdays,
Saturdays and Sundays 2.00-5.00 pm
Nature Reserve: daily 9.00 am-5.00 pm
Admission: free
Buses: 101, S1
BR stations: Manor Park, Woodgrange Park
Underground: East Ham
Exhibition of webs of life and food chains; nature trails through
4-hectare (9-acre) urban nature reserve maintained for
preservation of small animals, insects and birds.

INDEX

Page numbers shown in **bold type** refer to a main entry; those in *italics* show entries in the *Eating Out* and *Directory* sections.